DISCOVERING
YOUR SOUL
SIGNATURE

SPIEGEL & GRAU
NEW YORK

DISCOVERING YOUR SOUL SIGNATURE

A 33-DAY PATH TO
PURPOSE, PASSION & JOY

PANACHE DESAI

Published in the United States by Spiegel & Grau, Random House,
an imprint of Random House, a division of Random House LLC,
a Penguin Random House Company, New York.

SPIEGEL & GRAU and the HOUSE colophon are registered trademarks
of Random House LLC.

Library of Congress Cataloging-in-Publication Data
Desai, Panache.
Discovering your soul signature : a 33-day path to purpose, passion & joy /
by Panache Desai
pages cm
ISBN 978-0-8129-9558-9
ebook ISBN 978-0-8129-9559-6
1. Self-actualization (Psychology) 2. Self-realization. 3. Conduct of life.
I. Title.
BF637.S4D478 2014
158—dc23   2014001759

Printed in the United States of America on acid-free paper

www.spiegelandgrau.com

2 4 6 8 9 7 5 3 1

First Edition

To my beloved grandmother Shanti Desai,
my loving parents, Mira and Dilip,
my beautiful wife, Jan,
and my teachers—my daughters Olivia and Sophia.

The privilege of a lifetime is being who you are.
—JOSEPH CAMPBELL

Contents

Contents

Introduction

It is no accident that you're here. No accident that you've found your way to this page. Life has brought you to this precise moment—perhaps in the form of a divorce, a loss, a financial challenge. Maybe you've had a health scare. Or perhaps you have simply been awakened to a vague, indefinable yearning. This yearning exists inside you—a hunger, a subtle gnawing awareness that there is something more. Without even knowing it, you are touching upon a deep wish. It is your wish to find your most authentic expression.

Something about life the way you've been living it isn't quite working. Whether your challenges are large or small—whether your problems are visible or invisible—you are suffused with this yearning. I have news for you: *We all are.* To be human and to walk this planet is to experience a myriad of complex emotions.

So you are here. How you've gotten here no longer

matters. What is essential—in fact, miraculous—is the fact that you have made it.

Welcome! Your spirit has brought you to these words.

We do not choose the work we are brought into this lifetime to do. That work is your *soul signature*—your unique expression. Your spiritual DNA.

It is who you are at your core—your singular contribution to the world. It doesn't have to do with seeking fame or fortune—though it might—but rather with the accumulated essence of everything you have ever been, thought, felt, done, or experienced in your entire life.

By way of illustration, let me tell you how I discovered my own soul signature. As a very young boy, I spent every possible moment in the meditation room of my grandparents' home in East London. If I was fussy or having a tantrum, I calmed down the moment I crossed the threshold of that room. I sat there each morning and watched my grandmother pray. She chanted the Guru Gita, a devotional prayer to awaken the remembrance of the light within. My grandmother had beautiful long black hair and wore a sari. She smelled of coconut oil. She prayed for every one of us: for health, well-being, abundance. She closed her eyes and counted her mala beads. She read from the Mahabharata and the Bhagavad Gita. Devotional songs were always playing on a cassette player. The very air felt sacred in that room. Sacred, safe, profoundly loving, and strong. And though I didn't understand it at the time, it was the one place in the world where I felt at home.

For the first five years of my life, I existed in a pristine vibrational environment. The sole focus of everyone's attention was on the Divine.

And then it was gone.

My parents and I left that crowded home in East London when I was five years old, in search of better schools, a better way of life. I was an only child, solitary and shy. I felt absolutely disconnected from all that loving abundance I had been exposed to and wondered if I was being punished. How had I ended up in this extended "time-out"?

We moved a number of times subsequently. I went to two different middle schools. During my high school years, we wound up back in East London, in a poor, working-class neighborhood where everybody was just trying to get through the day. It was my introduction to feeling pain. I felt everything inside everybody. I felt all the fear-based and survival-based energy swirling around me. And even though we'd visit my grandparents on the weekends, the meditation room no longer called to me. I no longer felt its magic. I was a teenager and didn't really want to be spending Saturday nights meditating with a bunch of grown-ups.

I had no tools for the jungle of teenage life in East London. I was a sensitive, openhearted kid. I didn't understand why people were cruel to one another. People were beating each other up, everybody trying to dominate. Eventually—it had to happen—I got bullied. I didn't fit in with any group. I didn't tell my mom and dad what was happening. I cried myself to sleep some nights. I questioned why I was alive. What was the point?

The pain became great enough that I needed to find ways to numb it. I rejected my soul signature, moved away from my own unique expression of energy—and in so doing, I paid a price. In my late teens, I found my way into drugs, alcohol, and the music scene. I dropped out of university. I was like the proverbial frog in boiling water—everything around me growing hotter and hotter, more and more unmanageable, until I was dying, drowning without even knowing it. I had a radio show, ran raves and events as part of London's music scene, but the pain inside me was escalating. I had no interest in spirituality. I had completely stepped away from it. I stopped visiting my grandparents. The meditation room was like a figment of my past, an image from a long-lost dream. I couldn't picture it anymore. I couldn't possibly set foot in it.

In 2001, I received a wake-up call in the form of a fist-fight with three people in a local bar. One guy head-butted me, and they all piled on. Bouncers came over, and I got pulled out. Later that night, someone was shot. I was very lucky to be in one piece. That night—in a single moment—the drinking, the drugs, the music stopped. I was done. Tapped out. I recognized the blessing in what had happened. I also recognized that I had been given this lesson in a very mild way. If I hadn't heeded it—as happens in life—the lessons would have gotten louder, more dangerous and damaging.

Without exactly knowing how, I had an inchoate sense that I needed to find a way to connect once again with the energy I had connected with as a child. I needed, once again, to remember my soul signature.

There is no hierarchy when it comes to soul signatures. My soul signature has been a spiritual path. Yours might be inspiring children, coaching young people to fulfill their destiny, bringing your own unique set of gifts to bear on the world around you. As Dr. Martin Luther King once said, "If it falls your lot to be a street sweeper, sweep streets like Michelangelo painted pictures, sweep streets like Beethoven composed music, sweep streets like Shakespeare wrote poetry. Sweep streets so well that all the hosts of heaven and earth will have to pause and say: Here lived a great street sweeper who swept his job well." Your soul signature is authentically your own. Only you can share your particular soul signature on this earth. It is as individual as a fingerprint. Your soul signature resides at the deepest core of who you are and permeates every aspect of your life.

I knew that I had to go *home*, to a place where the energy was a match for me. I said goodbye to my parents and traveled to an ashram in the United States, where I stayed for six months. I performed selfless service, working in the kitchen, cooking giant vats of vegetarian food for hundreds of people on retreat. But I was a lousy yogi. I would go into the morning meditation and fall asleep in the meditation room, day after day. I would have failed guru school. I was angry, sad, lonely, and lost. All the emotions I had been stuffing for all those years came rising to the surface. But still, there was something deeply nurturing for me about being in the energy of that meditation room, because it reminded me of growing up. I could be at peace there.

When I left the ashram, I had no idea what was next. I was grateful for my time there, for the space to focus on myself and tap into my own emotions, but ashram life was not for me. It was an escape.

I was in my early twenties now and still longing for home. When I was in a place where I was in harmony with the energy, it was complete surrender, a profound physical and emotional relaxation. When I was in a place where the energy was out of whack for me, I felt insecure, overwhelmed, and frightened. I think this is true for all of us, only we don't realize what's going on. We don't attribute it to energy. We don't realize that we are out of alignment with our soul signature. We tend to blame ourselves and others.

Rootless, aimless, emotionally volatile, with no direction, no guidance, and no momentum, I made my way west from New York to Los Angeles. I was like a forest animal, sniffing my way to where I needed to be, operating on intuition and instinct. I found a small apartment in Venice, which I shared with a roommate. I went to a meditation center there, but it didn't feel like home either. I was waiting, though I didn't know what I was waiting for. I didn't realize that waiting had a function. The waiting *wasn't waiting*. It was working out everything going on inside myself. It was a pause. So often we mistake a pause for a misstep. But this wasn't a misstep. The pause was allowing everything false that I had accumulated over twenty-three years of life to crumble. I had begun to shed all of that *vibrational density*—a term you'll come to know well over the course of this book—at the ashram. All that grief, rejection, betrayal, loss, sorrow, rage, fear—a short lifetime's worth. And once I left the ashram, there was no escaping it. In fact, it began to amplify. It was confusing, because my old reality was bumping up against a new one. I could kind of see this new reality, way off in the distance. But I couldn't fully access it. Not yet.

On New Year's Eve of 2002, I was alone in my Venice apartment. My roommate had gone to see his family for the holidays. In this solitary, rootless place, I began to feel a wave of fear rising inside me. It was more intense than anything I'd felt before, and it wouldn't go away. Instead of receding, it was rising, rising. It felt as if there was another presence in the room. It was impossible to ignore. I tried to go to sleep early. There was no point staying up to watch the clock strike midnight! I was a basket case. I got out of bed, checked all the doors and windows to make sure that everything was locked. I even looked under the bed, like a little kid terrified of the bogeyman.

It seemed that all the terror I had ever felt in my life was inside me, washing over me in wave after wave. And along with these waves was something that felt like an electrical current. The more I felt the fear, the more the electricity increased. I now know that I was experiencing a complete vibrational overhaul, but I didn't have the language for this at the time. All I knew was that it seemed my world was ending. Which, in a way, it was.

I left my apartment, got into my car, and drove around L.A. for a while. But I couldn't outrun this thing. It was with me wherever I went. Finally, I drove back home and lay down on my bed with my palms open. I hadn't slept all night, and now it was morning. The energy seemed to concentrate itself in my heart. I wondered if I was having a heart attack. I was shaking and shaking—my identity falling away.

Finally, I surrendered. I just gave up. And the moment I did, the entire room filled from floor to ceiling with a golden light. I felt pinned to my bed by a feeling of electricity washing over me in a huge, swelling wave. The light was everywhere, so golden that it appeared to be almost white. The feeling associated with it poured over me and through me. I recognized it as love, but it was beyond any practical definition of the word *love*. As much as it was all around me, it was also inside me. My fear and sadness were gone. They had been systematically dismantled. This brilliant light, this love—I understood this completely—made up the building blocks of our reality. In the absence of fear, this light, this love, is what we would see all the time. I got up out of bed and walked out of my apartment and onto the streets of Venice. Everything was glowing—and I mean everything: the litter, the cars, the graffiti-covered walkways, even the drunk mariachi singer who always badly serenaded me outside my window. Luminosity filled everything and everyone. I was suddenly starving and went to have lunch at a Mexican restaurant. Even my burrito was luminous.

I thought then of my grandmother and the language of my childhood, her soft, gentle voice reading from the Hindu scriptures. The incense wafting through the meditation room. The morning rays of sunlight beaming through the windows. "The universe is the outpouring of the majesty of God, the auspicious one, radiant love. Every face you see belongs to him. He is present in everyone without exception." It was because of those early years listening to her pray that I was able to decipher and understand that I was experiencing the infinite nature of God.

I was here to be a messenger, I now understood. This was the very essence of me. My singularity. My soul signature. I had very nearly lost my way, but my soul signature had been waiting for me to discover it. And now, I knew, I would be aligned with it forevermore.

Being aligned with your soul signature ought to be the most natural thing in the world. And yet so many of us struggle. So many of us are unaware of the very existence of our soul signature. Being human, and filled to the brim with a complex swirl of human emotions, we tend to reject our true calling. We make it wrong.

Stop and ask yourself this question: Is it possible that, somewhere along the way, you have absorbed the message—whether delivered by your family, society, or your own insecurity—that *you are not enough*?

We turn our backs on the essence of who we are deep inside.

And, in so doing, we step directly into the experience of suffering and scarcity. We disconnect ourselves from our truest source. We become like baby chicks abandoned in the nest—not yet formed, in a weakened state, unable to feed ourselves, unable to fly. But when we are able to access and inhabit our own unique soul signature, we become complete. Acceptance of all we are allows our soul signature to amplify to its greatest expression. This occurs as a series of subtle shifts. Most of us do not experience this as fireworks going off. Rather, it's soft and surprising. The moment we are able to connect consciously with our soul signature—the moment we stop resisting the truth of our nature—our lives begin to change in ways we cannot even begin to imagine.

This book will take you on a thirty-three-day journey. You will undergo an intense process of peeling away layer after layer of trapped emotion that I call a Density Detox. This detox is designed to break the shell of all that has held you back. Through an unfolding series of systematic exercises and meditations, you will come into a detailed understanding and intimate knowledge of yourself. I will be asking you to embrace all the different aspects of you. Don't be frightened. I won't be asking too much of you. You don't have to go to an ashram, or eat kale, or drink strange potions.

In the morning, for just a few minutes, I will ask you to focus your attention on the emotions that have been blocking you. By gracefully and safely experiencing these emotions, you will begin to move through the blocks and limitations that have been keeping you from aligning yourself with your soul signature. By becoming willing to face yourself and all that you are, you will then gain access to the abundance and beauty, the awesomeness that is awaiting you.

At midday, I will ask you to pass through an experiential doorway that will allow you to test and apply your new awareness in your daily life—so that you don't just *know* it, you *live* it. With your new tools and awareness, you will begin to apply this awareness in a very grounded and concrete practical way. Through a series of personal insights and stories gleaned from my own experience and my work with people from around the world, I will share with you how to navigate your life with these newfound tools, a practice observed hour by hour, day by day.

And finally, in the evening, I will offer you a series of soulful meditations and lullabies designed to be read before bed. These will work on you even as you sleep—an emotional experience that reconnects you with the deepest knowing that is always inside you, a blanket that wraps itself around you and comforts you, reminding you of who you are at your core.

Ideally, you will want to go through all thirty-three days sequentially. If you commit to doing this in the order in which it was created, you will reap the greatest benefits. Some passages will resonate more than others. Sometimes, life will get in the way. If you find yourself unable to follow the thirty-three-day program straight through, don't beat yourself up about it! Allow your heart to be your gentle guide, because that is the essence of the soul signature. Trust in your heart. Open up to a page and read what's there. You will discover what you need.

We have all rejected ourselves in some way—rejected our soul signature—as I did as a young man. We have all endured painful and lonely times. This is part of the natural ebb and flow that everyone goes through in life. We're born into our soul signature. As teenagers, we often rebel against it. As young adults, we reject it because we believe in our own omnipotence. We look for love and acceptance in all the wrong places. Eventually—and you are here now—we give up that game and begin to embrace who we are, as we are. We begin to embrace the energy that created us. In so doing, life unfolds for us on every single level.

After all, there comes a point when you finally have to be good enough for you.

You being you is the blessing.

You being you is the miracle.

You being you is enough.

You being you is your soul signature.

A Note to the Reader

We are vibrational beings. We inhabit a vibrational universe. We have the appearance of solidity, but we aren't really solid. This is a scientific fact. Quantum physics has proven that energy can shift states from one form to another, that, ultimately, that which appears to be solid is actually composed of vibrating particles and molecules. Nothing is concrete. Everything is up for reconsideration. Everything! I am about to shift the way you look at your entire life.

As vibrational beings, when we experience emotions, those emotions are also made up of energy. *Emotions are just energy in motion.* When we repress our emotions or suppress our emotional content, whatever we are denying accumulates weight, or what I have come to call *vibrational density.* This heaviness can take many forms. But in all cases it impedes your spirit's natural ability to shine. Think of the way we sometimes describe our emotions: We stuff our anger. We hold back tears. We have a lump in our

throat. We gird our loins. We think we're protecting ourselves, but really what we're doing is keeping our optimal
selves behind a wall. We know there's more, but we don't
know how to get there.

Just as water has the ability to become ice, or to become steam, our energy, too, has the ability to shift states.
When we don't allow our emotions to flow, it's as if we're
filling ourselves with cement. We become so full of sadness, anger, guilt, fear, and shame that there is no room
left for anything else. The more encumbered we are, the
lower our rate of vibration—of connectedness, aliveness,
joy. The lighter we are—the more we've dealt with everything inside us—the more we are able to bring into our
lives abundance, health, love, and soulfulness.

This book will help you discover your soul signature.
The process begins by allowing your emotions to run
through you—to be the *energy in motion* that they are—so
that you can experience wholeness, oneness with the radiant energy, the pure love that the Divine has in store for
you.

In this very moment, you are calling into being your
greatest expression, your soul signature. Everything that
has ever happened in your life has served to bring you to
this place. This is the space in which you can receive the
truth that you are love. You are abundance. You are radiant health. You are profoundly connected to the Divine.
There is nothing—absolutely nothing—wrong with you.

You are poised to be able to live in absolute, uninterrupted connection with yourself.

You are not what you've been told. You've walked the journey you were meant to walk, and that journey has brought you here. Now it's time to dive into something greater. Something deeper and more expansive.

My greatest wish for you is that you come to be the love you are. And that you live that love in each moment of your life, from this day forward.

As I guide you through a safe and systematic dismantling of the emotions and thought processes that are holding you back from connecting with your soul signature, know that I am here to be your friend. This is a powerful, magical journey. Come. It's amazingly simple. I'm holding out a hand to you. Let's begin. I've been waiting for you all my life.

DISCOVERING
YOUR SOUL
SIGNATURE

Day 1 Fear

MORNING

There is a reason why we begin with fear. So often we allow fear to run our lives. Think about it. Nothing—absolutely nothing—is wrong, but something sets you off, and you start being fearful of something that hasn't happened and likely won't. Seemingly out of the clear blue sky, you start worrying about the bills. You start obsessing about your job. Maybe your boss doesn't really like you. Or maybe your coworker is sabotaging you. Your mind runs with this for a while. Possibly your fear takes the form of worry about your children. Johnny's B minus on a math test might be setting him up for a life of under-achievement. Sophie's been dealing with some middle school girl problems, and you worry that her self-esteem will be permanently damaged. Then, of course, there's always your health. You wake up in the morning with a headache, are sure it's a tumor. Before you know it, you've become a sick, unemployed, poor parent, *all in your mind.*

Whatever your particular fears are, they serve to constrict you and make your whole field of energy narrow.

Fear begets fear. Call to mind the image of a garden. What happens if we don't weed a garden? If we don't tend to it, our entire garden—all of those carefully cultivated rosebushes and peonies and daylilies—becomes overgrown. Roots become strangled, cut off from the source. Before you know it, all that beauty vanishes. *Fear is an energy.* It is an experience. But holding on to fear is unique to our human nature. Consider this: Every living being feels its fear and shakes it off. Cows, deer, fox, even bears—they all feel fear and move on. But we human beings don't. We accumulate fear. We hoard and store it in our bodies. We go out of our way to prove to ourselves that the world is not a safe place. Of course, there is an evolutionary place for fear—after all, it allows us to survive—but we let it run amok. And then it keeps us locked into place. Perhaps we stay in unsatisfying jobs or in bad relationships out of fear that something greater is not on its way. All the time we're doing that, we're invalidating the *universal principle of more.* The grass continues to grow. Rivers continue to flow into the sea. Galaxies are born. Life seemingly has a way of continuing to evolve into more. Everything in nature validates this principle.

We need to find our courage, which, of course, is not the absence of fear but rather the willingness to feel the fear and move forward anyway. Fear isn't going to kill us. It's an energy that we can allow to move through us.

Tend to the garden of your unconscious mind. Imagine yourself in a house surrounded by an absolutely beautiful garden. The only problem is that the garden has been overtaken by fear. Fear—of financial loss, of being alone, of illness, you name it—has taken the form of weeds. Go out of the house and tend to that garden. Visualize yourself on your knees, putting on your gardening gloves, pulling out your fear by its roots. What do we have here? Abandonment? Betrayal? Rejection? Death? It's all about the energy. This is a radical idea, I know—but your fears cannot hurt you. Pull out your first weed. The weeds *are your vibrational density.* Think of them as a mass of tangles. Dirty, all knotted up. What happens next? Here, your story doesn't matter. The specifics of who, what, where, when, and why are beside the point. You're pulling out the *energy* of fear. Just the energy—that's all. When that mass of tangles is uprooted, suddenly there's space. It won't necessarily feel comfortable. But stop for a minute. What *does* it feel like? Maybe there's a little more room now. Perhaps there's the beginning of new opportunity. In time, we will know. In giving fear our attention, it loses its power over us. The weeds aren't wrong or bad. They're just taking up space.

NOON

Perhaps you read the "Morning" passage while sitting at your kitchen table, grabbing a quick breakfast, a cup of coffee. Or maybe you were already on the train. Or in your car, driving to work as you listened to these words on an audiobook. Wherever you found yourself, I now want you to train your heart and mind—your awareness— on the energy of fear as it appears throughout your day. Each time today that fear arises within you—and make no mistake, it will arise—make note of it. *Fear is your ground zero.*

Typically, we manage our daily fears in one of three ways:

We run.
We stand our ground and fight.
Or we freeze.

You might be anticipating the homework assignment that requires you to read two hundred pages by tomorrow. Or the results of a pathology report. Or the business project that requires you to leave your wife and babies and travel halfway around the world to secure a contract. The first day of a new job. A first date. Opening a bill, terrified that you don't have the money to cover it. *Life and life situations will call us out on our fear, every single time.* And when this happens, the most primitive part of the brain takes over. The part of us that fights, flees, or freezes comes from our base animalistic response to the energy of fear. Everything in the natural world does this in the presence of fear. (Unless of course you're a possum, in which case you play dead.) This happens *whether or not there is a legitimate threat.* Our muscles contract. Our breathing becomes shallow. Our palms dampen. Our pupils enlarge. Our blood leaves our extremities and pools in the center.

So what do you do? You *learn to allow.* You have a familiar place you retreat to as a result of your fear. Get to know the place. Perhaps it's a set behavior, a pattern that you use to compensate for the presence of this uncomfortable energy. Maybe for you it's denial. Or egoic compensation. Arrogance. Distraction. Withdrawal. Introversion. The fridge. The bar.

We all have our survival mechanisms. For me, I go to that puffed-up place: *You're not going to mess with me.* I once again become that kid in London who had to develop bravado in order to survive. I can be in a business meeting, surrounded by people who know a lot more than I do about the subject at hand, but if I don't like the way things are going, I tend to fall back on false strength. I feel as if I need to be larger than life. This is an old way of adapting, of trying to survive. I have to learn, again and again, to catch myself in that behavior and stop. Trust. Notice. And allow the fear to run through me like a river out to sea.

So just for today, notice the special place you go when you start to experience fear. Does your ego begin to assert itself? Or do you want to hide? Do you reach for something to distract you? Do you become oblivious and shut down? Or do you try to numb it out? Do you reach for a cigarette, or your phone, or check your email for the five hundredth time? Or perhaps you'll choose not to engage. You'll pull the rug over your head and hope the moment passes.

Notice. Keep an eye out. It may happen only once today or a hundred times. It doesn't matter. There is immense power in the ability to catch yourself, to observe your own instinctive responses and behavior. And when you do notice, *meet yourself with absolute love.* The awareness signals the end of the fight. Not to say that your reptilian brain won't snake its way in a new direction. After all, that's what snakes do. But once you train your mind to notice what it's doing, fear will lose its stranglehold.

NIGHT

Until now, the invisible force of fear has been your constant companion. It has informed every decision and directed every choice. It is the knot in your heart that keeps you from fully loving. It has appeared at pivotal moments to steer you away from who you know you really are. It is the voice in your head telling you *no.* It is the very sound of defeat. It steals your birthright from you. It robs you of life itself.

Fear has served you well.

It has been your good old friend.

Until this very moment.

It's time.

As with a friend with whom you must part ways, it's time to say thank you. It's time to move on into a greater relationship, a greater receptivity, a greater expression. A greater truth. It's time to embrace the fear—old friend—and say goodbye. To say, *You have been with me for a long time. You have been the voice in my mind, to the point where I know no other. You have protected me and kept me safe. But you have served your purpose, and I must go. I choose to venture beyond your jurisdiction. I have the courage to walk into the unknown.*

Bow to your fear for all it has been, for all it has shown you. Picture again the beautiful garden you called to mind this morning. You and your fear are standing together in this garden. With a grateful heart, look around this garden. See an old, rusted gate. Slowly walk through this lush green garden to the gate and open the iron latch. As you pass through the gate, note the way it creaks closed behind you. The way the latch clicks shut. You are on a path now of uneven cobblestones, the greenery around you even more lush, flowers in full bloom. You hadn't even known this world existed, beyond these garden gates. As you walk down the path, pause for a moment. Turn around and look back. Are you having a moment of doubt? Who will you be in the absence of your good old friend? You don't know. You *can't* know. But you are willing to find out. Say goodbye to this energy of fear that kept you safe but small. Say goodbye to this energy that has kept you needy, that has weighed you down even as it has seemed to support you.

Notice that the garden is empty. Perhaps consider the possibility that it has always been empty. See? No one is there.

Day 2 Sadness

MORNING

Sadness is a heavier energy, lurking just beneath all that fear. Fear keeps the sadness locked in place, by preventing us from ever addressing, honestly and authentically, the fact that we don't want to feel our own broken hearts. It's a defense mechanism that keeps the sadness at bay. We don't want to open ourselves to our own sadness. Who wants to be that vulnerable? All that loss, that grief, that avalanche of sorrow? Why would we sign on for such a thing? So many times people tell me they're afraid that if they start feeling their sadness, they'll never stop crying.

But here is a radical idea: *The ability to be sad is a blessing.*

In our childhoods, we were taught that sadness is a sign of weakness. Remember your own childhood: Were you ever called a crybaby? Or made to feel ashamed of your tears? Did you somehow internalize the message that you were supposed to stuff those feelings, put on a brave face, chin up and all that? I'm here to tell you that if you want to release the vibrational density you're carrying around, you need to do the precise opposite. *Feel it. Feel it all.* What's the worst thing that can happen? When we allow ourselves to be vulnerable, *we are experiencing a blessing.* We are offering ourselves the opportunity to see and experience life authentically, without defenses or screens keeping us from our own true nature.

There is an exquisiteness to sadness and pain. It has a quality and resonance that is unique. It's a way we all can relate to one another, because we all feel sadness. Were it not for our judgment of that emotion, no one would have a problem feeling it. Sadness is socially unacceptable—we're conditioned from day one to understand sadness as a sign of weakness—so people refuse to experience it, and it accumulates weight. Its density grows in the body. Look at the body language and posture of someone who is experiencing a depression: They seem to carry a weight on their shoulders. They're hunched over. They can hardly get out of bed. It's like a weeping willow tree as opposed to a mighty oak. The oak tree is firm and elegant and upright. The weeping willow has allowed the burdens of life to bend it.

The key is to shift your experience of sadness. Grief? Loss? Tears pouring down your cheeks? *Good.* Feel it all. Know that you are one of 7.2 billion people on this planet who experience the same thing. The rejection of sadness further separates you from your own wholeness. Lean into it. Breathe. Accept. Embrace and embody the blessing of sadness, because where there is acceptance, judgment no longer has any power. When you let this energy wash over you, there will be an intensity to it, but as you keep allowing it to flow through you, it will eventually diminish. Allow life to do its job.

NOON

As the Buddha said, life is suffering. But there is magnificence in that suffering. And what's more, *there is no true turning away from it*. It is in turning *toward* suffering that, paradoxically, we discover our most vivid, alive, electric, feeling, sensitive, sensual selves.

When sadness arises within us, we are being given an incredible opportunity to integrate the wounds of the past. We are being allowed to experience the very fabric of our story. Perhaps you woke up this morning and, for no reason, seemingly out of the blue, you felt sad. Your natural tendency would be to tighten up in the face of it. Buck up, old chap. Think about the way we cry. Either we stuff our tears and swallow the lump in our throats, or we allow our tears, which stream down our faces, real and true and irrefutable.

Take a moment and put down your cup of coffee. Unless you're driving, close your eyes. Feel the swells rising and falling within you. Riding those swells is a feeling you like to keep at bay. What would happen if you felt it? Envision it as a tiny boat, tossed about by the crests of the waves that are always inside you. That boat is an intricate thing of great value and beauty. It is honed and colored by what it means to have been given this precious gift of life.

I am asking that, as you move through your day, you allow life to impact you. When you see a young child reaching for his mother's hand, allow your heart to open. When you see someone struggling in the street, allow your heart to open. When you receive a disappointment or a setback, allow your heart to open. This is the exquisite doorway through which life becomes larger and richer. *Your sadness doesn't make you less of a human being.* In fact, it makes you more.

More expansive.

More connected.

Painfully beautiful.

Raw. Open. Completely alive.

Allow life to touch you. And when life touches you, meet it with softness. Meet it with authenticity. Allow your heart to merge with the hearts of people around you. See yourself in the faces of your fellow human beings. Just for today, live in the truth that *there is nothing to defend.* Live in the truth that *vulnerability is power.* Live in the truth that your sadness makes you human. As you leave for work, your child calls out, "Bye, Daddy! I'm going to miss you!" Feel it. Allow your heart to break open. As you drop your older child off at school, notice the mother walking her disabled eight-year-old through the school's front doors. Don't look away. Feel it. Feel it as if that is you—

because *it is you.* When you stop at the market, notice the elderly couple shopping together. They've been married for sixty years and are still holding hands. Feel it. This, too, is you. Drive past the cemetery where your parents are buried. Look out at the thousands of tombstones, the lives once lived. Feel them. Feel them all.

These feelings are not going to kill you.

In fact, these feelings are going to connect you.

To your own story, and to the stories of others.

Allow. Just for today, allow all that sadness in. Whenever you feel your heart, your body, or your mind hardening against what you're seeing, soften. Relax your belly. Breathe into your heart. Become aware of the soft and tender place that is always inside you, like a pilot light, softly burning. That light is waiting for a moment of conscious recognition. Receive these moments. Experience them. Live the blessing of your exquisite life.

NIGHT

I am the tears you will not shed. I am the result of a life unlived. I am the experience of trying to please everyone else. I am the feeling of being lost. I am inconsolable. I am the part of you that you will not put on display, for fear that I may quickly turn into a raging river. For fear that I might drown you. I am the part of you that you always keep in check. I am your secret lover. I share space with you on your pillow at night. I am present in your heartbreak. I am present in your loss. The accumulation of me leads to your grief. Without me, you would be lost.

I reside in your lungs. I suffocate you from within. When I arise, a tight pressure and viselike grip surrounds your neck, encircles your throat.

I render you mute.

I steal your voice.

You're all choked up.

You will do everything you can to push me away. You will drink. Smoke. Have sex. Overeat. You'll try to outrun me, only to discover that you cannot. I linger within you. *I linger within all of us.* Moments of vulnerability expose my presence. Relationships draw me up and out. I reach a point when you no longer can contain me. When you no longer can hide me. When you have no choice but to admit that I exist.

I am real.

I am here.

I am a part of you.

You can run no more—and it's *okay.*

I was present at the birth of your children. I was present at the death of your mother. I was present in the moment of abuse and trauma. I was present when the world rejected and shunned you. I was present on the playground. In the cafeteria. In the locker room. I was there when the news headlines reported the tragedy: the gunned-down children, planes flying into buildings, young girls sold into sexual slavery. I was the uninvited guest at your wedding. I was there at your child's graduation. At the death of the family dog. At the birth of your grandchildren. The loss of your wife. The ringing phone. The officer at the door. In the hospital. On the cold, cold ground. I have been there every step of the way.

I am your sadness.

I am your tears. I am your grief. Your loss. I am *you*. I will exist until your last breath. To be in human form is to feel me.

Allow the dam to break. I need to move through you. Come home to me. Come here. I have something to show you.

Come.

I have been waiting for you.

Allow me to lead you home.

Open to me. Allow me to flow. Allow the stream of me to move through you freely. I need to be free. Don't be afraid of me. Allow me to go. I must go now. Don't worry—I'll be back. I can never really leave. You will always feel me—but feel me like the wind on your back, or the lake surrounding you, the simple air you breathe. I always want to be moving. I always want to be in motion. Don't hold me back. It only hurts both of us.

Let me go.

Let me go.

Day 3 Anger

MORNING

I love anger. Angry people are just more-empowered sad people. Call to mind the last time you were really, truly angry. Feel what was happening in your body: those waves and waves of energy, your blood boiling, your vision acute and pointed, fingers tingling. Anger is a great energy. Fantastic! If enough people on the planet get pissed off about something, it often changes. The energy of rage can be enormously positive—except, of course, when it is coupled with extreme judgment and perverts itself into acts of terror and war. Instead of tamping anger down, let it flow. Let it run through your being like a bolt of electricity from head to toe.

As the energy rises, meet it. Allow it to move through you. It's the repression and suppression of it that leads to a distorted, destructive place. To my mind's eye, anger looks and feels almost like a volcano. When it erupts inside us and we remain neutral, we are able to feel it in a fluid way, and nothing gets stuck. We learn to recognize our anger consciously as it begins to rise. We allow it to unfurl inside ourselves. If we're fully open to it, we can allow it to flow through us. Our natural tendency is for anger to get stuck: in the throat, in the gut, in the jaw. For some of us, the idea of releasing this anger can be scary. We're afraid of our anger's effect. Maybe we've seen up close what anger, unleashed, can look like—and it hasn't been pretty. But in allowing it to move through us, we are giving this energy a chance to run its course. Think of what happens when you're in a car and you shift that car into neutral. When you're in neutral, you can rev the engine to your heart's content and you don't run anyone over, you don't crash into anything.

This takes a level of awareness. When I start to feel the emotion of rage, first I take a moment to recognize it. I breathe and relax instead of contracting in the presence of it. Then I can begin to feel it in my body, bubbling up. It moves through me. It's a bit like being one of those cartoon characters with smoke coming out of their ears—and then it's over. It's moved on through. No one has been harmed in the process—including myself.

It's only when we direct that energy *at* someone that it becomes destructive—because in truth, the anger we experience is our own. We're angry because we're angry, and whatever happened that brought it up is actually the blessing—because ultimately, the more we're available to experience it, the more it comes into balance.

Try expressing your anger creatively. Move your body. Anger loves a physical release. Breathe deeply. Punch the hell out of your pillow. Scream as loudly as you can into that pillow—scream until your throat is raw. Why not? Journal it. Spew it all into your journal, and if you need to write *I'm pissed off* for ten pages straight, do that. There is a physical component to anger. It's a visceral, powerful energy. Witness it and feel it, but don't add to the anger quota of the universe. When that volcano goes off in your body, slow down. Begin to breathe slowly, feel the molten lava . . . The more you allow for this eruption to happen, the more you will see that it will flow through you and disappear. Ironically enough, when you have finally moved through your anger, the feeling you will be left with is one of strength and empowerment.

NOON

Maybe you're reading this on your phone while standing on line at Starbucks, waiting to order your double-shot vanilla latte, and all of a sudden someone cuts in line. Do you say anything? No, probably not. But the sleeping dragon deep inside your chest stirs a bit. Then you get into your brand-new car, which you just picked up from the dealer last week. The car next to you has parked too close, and now there's a scratch on your driver's side door. The dragon lifts its head. Now you're driving. You're late for work. An old person in front of you is driving well below the speed limit. You know you should feel empathy. You know that someday you, too, will be an old person. But, instead, you're all revved up. The dragon shakes its tail. You've arrived at the office. They've started the meeting without you and are discussing your proposal. The dragon lets out a puffy breath of fire. You feel it in your body. The heat. The pounding heart. The head rush. Blood coloring your face. You're off to the races now. The rest of your day is informed by this anger. Unless—unless you discover a different way of processing it and understanding it.

I'm hoping your morning hasn't already gone in this direction. I hope you're still calmly and quietly contemplating the day ahead. As you contemplate, I'm going to ask you to make the focus of your day *honesty*. The person cutting in line at Starbucks is not making you angry. Neither is the bad parker or the old person. Nor are your colleagues. *The sleeping dragon is already there.* We must acknowledge that our anger is a part of us. Our natural tendency is to make it about the person who cut the line or scratched the car. But we need to develop the awareness that *we are not the victims of what's happening*. In fact, we are being presented with a valuable opportunity to use what is happening as a catalyst to free ourselves from our normal state of reactivity.

How often in life is it true that the only person in the room who knows you are angry is you?

We don't know what to do with our anger. We're afraid

of it. Therefore, it disempowers us. Most of us haven't had anger modeled for us in a way that is positive. We've only seen it be destructive. Too often, we wait until it's too late, and we've either given ourselves an ulcer or smashed everything to bits.

As you move through your day, some version of any of the scenarios I listed above will happen. You'll get pissed off thirty different times. Why would you—why would any of us—be exempt from this? We're human, after all. I still end up losing it with people. I have my own triggers—I am at my most susceptible when I feel as if I'm being disrespected or demeaned. Because I was bullied as a kid, being disrespected sets off my dragon—which is not any ordinary dragon that just wants to breathe fire. It's a bad-ass dragon that wants to chew your head off and then keep your skull as a souvenir to wear around its neck. No matter how much I open up emotionally and embrace all there is, this can still happen in my life. For the most part, after years of hard work and self-examination, I've learned to feel my anger. I've had to rewire myself—because the hard wiring of my childhood led to this particular vulnerability. We make progress, but this doesn't mean we're not going to feel things!

When anger starts to arise, the first thing you need to do is *catch yourself in the experience*. Realize what's happening. Note it. Feel it in your body. Where is it? When you've located it, breathe and relax. Don't pretend it's not there. In fact, completely recognize that it's there. Let it run through you. We need to meet our own inner dragon with love. Feel it moving from your stomach, up and out, just like the fire breath of that dragon. Notice, as your day goes on, how often you might need to do this. That's fine. That's good! You're not accumulating anger now. You're addressing it fully in each and every moment. You're catching and releasing it, the way a fisherman might catch a fish, then toss it back into the stream. No pretending, no stuffing, no reacting. Watch yourself, and see what happens. That's freedom, right there.

NIGHT

A wrong look. The wrong word. Rush-hour traffic. The annoying colleague. Someone censors you. Cuts you off. Tries to stop you from being who you are. You feel limited. Insulted. Betrayed. Pent-up energy builds and builds. And then—from a place so primal, so preverbal that you can't even articulate it—mayhem and chaos are unleashed with such a force that everything and everyone around you is covered in ash. Scalded and burned.

There is a furnace burning within you. A volatile, powerful dissonance. If left unexplored, it can lead to dark and dire places. These churning, unrelenting flames are caused by a lifetime of not speaking up. A lifetime of being pushed around. A lifetime of not being *seen*. Of not being heard. Your passivity in the face of your own futility has led to the accumulation of this raging, bellowing fire that is all-consuming, pervasive, and colors every single moment of your life.

It started off as resentment.

It quickly escalated into frustration.

Over the years, it built and built into anger.

And, left unexpressed, now it has become rage.

Rage seeks its own liberation. It has its own agenda. Once it has found form, we no longer have any control over it. That's when we lose it! Think of it as bright, red hot, molten at its core. Flickers of yellow and orange sparks fly off in every direction. It is surrounded by waves of heat. It is always there, quietly waiting. Circumstances have to be right. An opportune moment and—*wham!*—it will explode.

Here is what the Divine would like to say to you: *I understand your anger. I understand your rage. I understand your resentment. I completely and fully understand your frustration. I understand this volatile and yet beautiful part of you. The part of you you've been taught to condemn. The part you've been taught to repress. This part of you is profoundly human. This part of you has a place. It belongs, just as much as every other part of you.*

It's not wrong. It's okay. You can relax. Your anger doesn't make you any less of a person. You're no less spiritual, no less loving because of it. In fact, its presence adds a dimension to you that is really quite endearing. Think of a two-year-old having a tantrum: The beet-red face. The eyes squeezed shut. The mouth open in a wail. Have you ever watched a two-year-old having a tantrum and then had to stop yourself from laughing? You think your anger makes you ugly, but it doesn't.

It only makes you human.

Anger is an energy like any other. Remember: Emotion is just energy in motion. As you put this book down and drift off to sleep, know that your anger is welcome here. Your anger is welcome. It has a place. Be available to it. Stop hurting yourself by suppressing it. Stop girding yourself. You can feel it without exploding. Without hurting yourself or anyone else. Unclench your fists. Release your jaw. You're going to close your eyes in a moment. Take three deep breaths. Open up the doors and let the lava gently flow as you sleep.

Dream your anger.

Dream it.

Awake in peace.

Day 4 Guilt

MORNING

The palm trees near my house in Florida are regularly attacked by an insect called whitefly. Whitefly creates this sticky saplike residue that drips onto everything surrounding it. These insects ruin everything they touch. Guilt is a lot like this. People who are riddled with guilt don't dare to be abundant or happy because they fundamentally believe that something they did was heinous. But they are thinking only of their past selves. They forget that they were *only operating from the awareness that they had at the time.*

Guilt is an insidious energy, because it eats away at people. Sometimes the guilt isn't even yours. It's something that has been conditioned into you by your parents or perhaps by a religious institution. Our inner worlds are often filled with thoughts about ways that we've messed up. Perhaps we've messed up by standing by while something terrible happens to someone else. Or we've cheated in some way, or lied, or strayed. Whatever it is, that guilt accumulates density in us as we hold on to it. Twenty years later, we're still lugging all these stories around like so much baggage. They weigh us down and get in the way of our evolution.

Guilt impedes our ability to receive everything that life offers us. If life presents us with relationships, opportunity, money, we will sabotage them because we feel unworthy. We'll punish ourselves, all the while having no idea why we're doing so. Guilt locks the reality of unworthiness in place. It can tie up generations. Guilt in a family lineage is like a piece of rope that stretches through time.

But we can break the cycle. It isn't that we ever want to forget what has happened or sanction what has occurred. But we can place guilt in its proper perspective.

Gather up the guilty parts of yourself. Embrace them. Call to mind something you feel terribly guilty about. It can be anything you're holding on to—from that candy bar you stole from the corner store as a kid, all the way to the affair you had or wanted to have. Recognize the distance between then and now. The evolution that comes with time allows for an increased awareness. Allow the underlying energy that is holding the guilt in place to arise. *That energy is almost always sadness.* Feel it. Feel it all. Know that the Divine doesn't judge you. The Divine is filled with nothing but love. Look back at your past self with this same love. Allow far more spaciousness than you had when you were in the midst of whatever you're holding on to. You cannot hold yourself hostage. All you can do is meet that younger, less evolved version of yourself with compassion and equanimity. After all, at this moment—today—you would do things differently if you could. So hug yourself. Hold yourself. And let it go. It's okay for you to move on.

NOON

If you're like most human beings, you wake up in the morning and—whether you're conscious of it or not—you make certain promises to yourself. You're going to be kind and caring to your loved ones. You're going to be a better member of society. You're going to stick to your diet. You're going to forgo that glass of wine with dinner. You aren't going to yell at your kid. You're going to balance your checkbook once and for all. And . . . what happens? Most of the time, we break those promises to ourselves.

In fact, I did this just yesterday! Lately I've been on a diet, and yet I ate a second plate of food. Why? I thought I was still hungry. I was feeling deprived. Or maybe I was stuffing my face instead of dealing with my feelings. Whatever the reason, once this happened, I felt bad. Angry that I let myself down. Sad that I had broken my own promise. Fearful that this would be the beginning of a slippery slope ending with my weighing three hundred pounds. And this potent stew of anger, sadness, and fear started bubbling in my own internal Crock-Pot, flavors mingling, and became an energy that *actually doesn't exist on the scale of human emotion.*

Guilt.

We are not born with guilt. It is not natural to us. Rather, guilt is a learned and conditioned response to what happens when we violate our own inner integrity. Today is dedicated to the energy of guilt. As you move through your day, you will notice this feeling arising. It can be subtle, and you may not be able to name it right away—because, remember, guilt is not organic to our very beings. Rather, it is a bellwether, a warning sign, *the Divine's way of letting us know that we're drifting out of alignment.*

Do you remember, back when you were a kid, that time that you stuck gum under your desk when no one was looking? Okay, maybe you didn't do exactly that. But you did *something*. As adults we have hundreds of versions of this. We eat ice cream straight out of the container. We tell a fib. We gossip about a close friend. We wear a sweater with the tags still attached, then return it to the store. We know—even when we're in the midst of these moments— that we are not in alignment with our best selves. And in the gap between our behavior and who we want to be— that is where guilt makes itself known.

When this happens, we are being given an incredible opportunity to see ourselves clearly and to grow.

When you are faced with a moment in which you've

broken your promise to yourself and guilt rises up, it may not present itself as guilt with a capital G. This energy may disguise itself—it may morph into defensiveness or self-justification. (You know: It was just a small lie. It didn't hurt anyone. The store won't notice.) We'll do anything to avoid the emotional impact of what's really going on.

Of course you won't want to sit with your guilt! The ramifications are so painful, none of us want to face our own broken promises. But during the course of this day, stop yourself each time you feel this subtle energy arise. Be clear, honest, and available. Understand it as a precious tool, a guide that will lead you back to your higher self, your own unerring internal compass. Over time, this compass will help to point you in the right direction.

NIGHT

You weren't born guilty. You weren't born encumbered. The thick molasses of guilt has slowly seeped into you over the years, filling you bit by bit until you are overflowing with it. Close your eyes and feel this energy for a moment. Gooey. Sticky. Once it touches you, it's hard to free yourself. Your every effort to escape it leaves you further mired.

You're a bad person. You don't deserve what you have. You could have handled things differently. You're unworthy. You said the wrong thing. *Did* the wrong thing. Feel it in your stomach. This is where guilt lives. It can feel like an intense nausea. It is, in fact, a poison, a toxic, malevolent substance that has attacked you from the outside in.

Guilt is a self-inflicted wound.

But it isn't a lethal wound.

Let us begin by feeling the wound. An arrow pierces your skin. You feel a heaviness washing over you. The affair you had. The lie you told. You screamed at your child. You didn't call your mother. You gossiped maliciously. You betrayed a friend.

I'm imagining you're reading this in bed, this book balanced on your chest or your e-reader glowing in the dark. Lie still and feel this arrow. Maybe there's more than one. Maybe you're covered in them.

Tell me. Can you take any of it back?

Can you bend time and go back to whatever you did and do it differently? No. The fact is, you can't.

But that isn't cause for despair or a sense of futility. Instead, you are being presented with a valuable opportunity. To grow. To transform. To soften. To forgive. To accept. Self-acceptance is the powerful antidote to these poison arrows. When you are filled with the elixir of self-love, no poison can harm you. Gently take hold of these arrows and pull them from your body. Know that scars will remain. Your skin has been broken. You will forever carry with you the memory of guilt, which is not the same as guilt itself.

In time, the scars will fade. The stories will lose their charge. They have become part of your greater story. A piece of the puzzle of what brought you to this moment.

Love yourself whole.

Love yourself, scars and all.

By loving yourself in this way, you are loving all who have ever been wounded in the same ways. You are embracing humanity just as the Divine intends.

The arrows are gone, the poison rendered useless. As you drift off to sleep, send love to each and every one of these scars. They are your teachers.

Day 5 Shame

MORNING

Shame and guilt are both born of judgment, but there is a distinction between them: Shame is silent. We wear our guilt—and we hide our shame. We'll share our guilt—it's a way in which we look for acceptance. We purge ourselves—telling our best friend, our sister or brother; we confess our supposed sins to God or to clergy. But we don't share our shame. Instead, we lock it away in a dark closet where we hope it will never be revealed, but all the while it is shaping our lives.

Because that which we do not bring into the light of day controls us.

Shame can be about anything, from our choice of sexual expression—if you ever want to clear a room, just start talking about sex—to our bodies, our addictions, our secret thoughts. Sometimes it comes from having an embarrassment of riches—a person born into a privileged family may feel ashamed about that. It manifests in so many different forms. As they say in twelve-step programs, it's cunning, baffling, and powerful.

Shame leads to isolation. The antidote for shame is intimacy. *Authentic vulnerability.* These emotional states are one and the same. In order to be truly intimate with another person, we must be authentically vulnerable. In addition, when we reach that place of vulnerability, we are also able to receive—truly receive—from another. When we express all that we are, there is no room for shame to creep in. This willingness to be honest, even if at times it's uncomfortable, is how we release the shame within us, so that it can no longer gather weight and density.

Look into your own eyes in the mirror. Just relax and breathe. Maintain your gaze. See the part of you that is sacred. See your soul. See the truth of you. Witness the part of yourself that cannot be tarnished. The simple part of you that is free of the complexities of life. From this place of intimacy with yourself, speak the truth that cannot be spoken. Your deepest shame. I promise you that this deep shame is shared by every single human being. By voicing it, you are letting it go. By remaining silent, you are feeding it, allowing it to increase in density. Alone in a room, allow for the huge breaking open of the dam you've created because you believe you're awful. You are not alone. We think we're alone in our awfulness, but we're not. In fact, we're not awful. We're one and the same.

NOON

Perhaps when you read the title of this chapter you thought, *That's not for me.* Even the word *shame* feels shameful. The more you have a visceral response—the more you want to skip over this chapter—the more you actually need it.

You might be thinking, *Who, me? I don't feel shame. I've worked through all that.* But shame is insidious. It doesn't present itself in neon lights. In your daily life, it won't manifest as shame. What it will feel like—and I'll bet this is something you've felt on a regular basis—is unworthiness.

That's right. Unworthiness.

Now do I have your committed attention?

A friend or a colleague pays you a compliment. Your sister says something kind about you. Your boyfriend buys you flowers. And . . . you can't receive it. You can't take it in. Your very body language is to back away. To duck your head, gesture with your hands—pushing the compliment away. *No, no,* you'll mumble. Maybe you'll blush. You'll go a little emotionally numb. You'll feel embarrassment.

This is shame at work.

Shame is the undercurrent that keeps you living in the belief that you are unworthy of all the bounty life has to offer.

Somewhere along the way, we have internalized the belief that we are—in our deepest selves—defective and wrong. *Shame is not a natural human emotion.* Babies aren't born feeling shame. We manufacture it within ourselves, as punishment for not adhering to the norms of society. But here is a provocative idea. If we feel shame for our private thoughts and actions—we do not know, *we cannot know*, other people's private thoughts and actions, so we compare our insides to other folks' outsides—we don't allow ourselves the life-altering knowledge that *we are so far from alone.* Our innermost expressions, thoughts, and behavior are the true norm. Only we don't talk about it. Shame keeps each of us in our own dark closet—hidden from the light of day.

In our day-to-day experience, the key to recognizing the energy of shame is to *catch yourself when you are deflecting.* This happened to me recently in a way so stark I couldn't ignore it. After a retreat I led in Chicago, a woman came up to me and told me that before she arrived at my retreat, she had been on the verge of suicide. Now she had a renewed sense of life. She began to cry—and in that moment it was impossible for me to take in what she was saying. I couldn't receive from her. I went through the motions but lost the sacred opportunity to meet another human being, soul-to-soul, who was telling me that I had made a difference. Deep inside myself, I was deflecting wildly. *Who me? No, not me.*

As you move through this day—this one precious day—be aware of each time you deflect. Each time you defend yourself. It may manifest as squeamishness. Discomfort. Embarrassment. A desire to flee. You might even self-consciously laugh. Do you know that nervous smile or giggle? That's deflection, right there. Notice how much easier it is, during the course of your day, to receive blame and criticism rather than kindness and praise.

When you catch yourself deflecting, stop. Breathe into your heart. Open your palms. Just this simple gesture will allow you to begin to receive the love, the support, the help, the praise, the small act of kindness. Someone offers you his seat on the train. Or just smiles at you as you pass. We feel so awkward when someone smiles at us, don't we? Our inner chatter, if we could really hear it, would be this: *Oh God, you can't be smiling at me. If you knew what I was hiding inside myself, you wouldn't smile at me . . .*

Our shame deems us unlovable.

It prevents us from asking for help.

It keeps us stuck and spinning in the same old story.

Just for today, step into receptivity. Your deflection is your road map. Pull yourself out of the invisible vortex of shame that has become your default setting.

Just for today, see what it feels like to open those clenched fists—that clenched heart—and receive every good thing.

NIGHT

I am your secret. I am the thing you do when nobody's around. I am your guilty pleasure. The part of yourself that you can't bear to admit. You keep me locked away, hidden from view. You're so afraid what the world will think if you're exposed.

I am your escape.

Your twisted companion.

Your refuge.

Your love.

I'm the source of your confession—or perhaps you don't even confess me. I am your confusion and your conflict. Your inner battle. I am your pornography. Your hidden sexuality. Your nightly joint. Your bottles hidden under the sink. I am your shopping. Your credit-card debt. Your sleeping pills. Your snooping. I am everything you crave and abhor.

I am your shame.

You believe I set you apart. That no one else feels as you do. That no one else *does* as you do. That your secret life is unique and ugly and yours alone. When you are in my grip, you can hear doors slamming shut. You can see bars on the windows. You have built your own prison, with me as its walls. Whenever I am on the verge of being freed—liberated, introduced to everyone in your life— you won't. You can't. You're afraid that if people knew about me, they would shun you. They wouldn't understand. They would point their fingers at you and laugh. Or worse. And so you hold on to me for dear life.

I'll tell you a secret.

There is only one way to begin to loosen my grip on

you. Admit that I exist. Say my name out loud. You know you want to, even though it's scary. You can whisper it. Do it right now. With your head on the pillow, give me a voice. No one will hear. Understand that, even if they did, it wouldn't matter. They would understand, because they, too, are acquainted with me.

Shine light on me.

Don't be frightened.

What you will discover is this: *You are not alone.*

When you become aware that you are one among the multitudes, that to be human is to feel me, that is when I will loosen my grip on you.

That is when I will finally let you go.

Day 6 Self-Judgment

MORNING

I'm stupid. Ugly. Fat. Unlovable. I'm an idiot. Boring. I don't deserve happiness or pleasure. Yada yada yada. This is how many of us talk to ourselves all the time, twenty-four hours a day, even when we're dreaming. It's like we've internalized our very own Judge Judy, who has taken up residence in our heads and is speaking into a megaphone. It's our own personal courtroom of persecution and self-flagellation. No audience is required.

And then we wonder why our reality obliges. We speak to ourselves in a way we wouldn't speak to our worst enemy. And because we exist in a vibrational reality—one in which all of life responds and resonates with our emotional states—it is an absolute guarantee that any and all judgments, criticisms, and evaluations that we place on ourselves will be echoed right back to us.

The evidence that your mind is creating is false. When

you were in third grade, perhaps your teacher told you that you'd never write legibly in your life, so your mind leapt to the judgment: *I'm stupid.* A boyfriend rejected you when you were twenty, and you decided: *I'm not sexually attractive.* Your father and mother divorced when you were a kid, and somehow this translated as: *I'm unworthy.* These are stories you tell yourself, stories that are entirely your own invention, and yet *because you are the author of them*, they are running your life.

Self-judgment is a mental affliction. Through self-judgment, people are living in their own private hell, every single day.

The doorway out of judgment is acceptance. Acceptance serves as a bridge between the mind and the heart. When we accept ourselves instead of internalizing circumstances and opinions that have nothing to do with the reality of who we are, once again the underlying energy is able to flow. But when we judge ourselves, we lock that energy in place.

What would happen if today—right now—you were to accept one thing that you've judged yourself—or been judged—for. Your fat thighs, for instance. That time you failed your driver's ed test. Stop believing your old stories. Those narratives likely no longer apply. And even if they do, judging yourself creates vibrational density and stops the energy that wants to do what energy wants to do: expand and flow. Sometimes, when I'm leading a live program, I will have a roomful of hundreds of women stand and put their hands on their butts. I ask them to repeat: *I love my butt*. When they begin, they're shy, embarrassed, tentative. Mortified, really. But still they continue. With each repetition, the density dissipates. If you were to walk into that room a little while into the exercise, what you would see is a roomful of proud, glowing goddesses, hands on butts, feeling empowered, sexy, and awesome.

No doubt, your list of self-judgments is long, but just pick one. It doesn't have to be your butt. Whatever it is, turn your self-judgment into acceptance by giving it a voice. Take a baby step.

NOON

Perhaps you read the "Morning" passage on "Self-Judgment" while you were still sleepy, shaking off the remnants of a dream, not yet encumbered by the day ahead.

Your mind was quiet, peaceful, spacious.

And then your day began.

Your first cup of coffee. A minor tiff with your wife. Going head-to-head with your teenager about last night's homework. Checking your email. The newspaper headlines. The day ahead. And then along came a voice—maybe a whisper, maybe a shout—that started the cycle of self-recrimination that, *whether you're conscious of it or not*, is your constant companion.

I'm always exhausted and stressed out.
I'm never going to get a raise.
I'm destined to be stuck in a cubicle.
Always a bridesmaid, never the bride.

Wherever your particular vulnerabilities lie, this judging voice knows where to find them and how to rip off the scabs covering the wounds within you, thereby always keeping those wounds fresh and bleeding.

Today I'm going to lovingly suggest that you become very aware of this voice. You'll have to be vigilant, because it will assume many disguises. Sometimes it can seem to be telling you for your own good. It can be quite convincing. Other times it's so soft and subtle that it can seem as if it's just the music that always fills your ears, a low, steady hum of self-judgment.

Life's circumstances set it off—and since circumstances are always shifting and changing, the nature of this judgmental voice will also shift and change. *When the voice of self-judgment is present, it is a surefire trigger for vibrational density.*

This morning I was taking a run near my home in Florida. I was about fifteen blocks from my house—running with a buddy—and suddenly my legs started to get heavy. I thought I wouldn't make it home. My inner judge had already tried and convicted me of failure before I even knew what was happening. Running is a relatively new activity for me, and at that moment every fiber of my being was telling me that running was ridiculous, that *I* was ridiculous. My knees hurt. I was out in the blazing hot sun. Who did I think I was? An athlete? I'm just a chubby kid from East London.

I completely bought into this internal monologue. I felt defeated. But then my friend reminded me that I've made it home before. That—no matter what—I'd make it back to my house. By removing myself from the chatter in my head and instead listening to my running companion, I was suddenly energized. The magnetic pull of the destructive inner monologue—the monologue that seemed to be adding twenty-pound weights to my ankles—was neutralized.

Our inner monologues have tremendous power over us. They can affect not only our mood, not only our physical bodies, but also our every waking moment—and, therefore, every consequence.

At some point today, you will find yourself in the midst of a self-judgmental cycle. If you're anything like the rest of us, it will happen multiple times. Stop and examine what's really going on underneath. *What is the vibrational density beneath the chatter?* Is it sadness? Anger? Fear? Shame? Take a moment and unpack it for yourself. Don't make the chatter real and let it stop you. It isn't real. The danger of self-judgment is that it can stop us from going beyond it. So what's driving it? If I had stopped in the blazing hot sun this morning and succumbed to the judgmental voice shouting that I'm nothing but a failure, two things would have happened: First, the voice would have won. But, more important, I wouldn't have been able to access the fear and sadness beneath it.

You see, during my run, I recognized those twenty-pound ankle weights as fear and a certain type of sadness that visits me when I step outside my comfort zone—therefore I was able to begin the process of experiencing the energy that kept that debilitating belief in place. Once I experienced the energy, it began to dissolve. And I was able to run the rest of the way home.

Without the energy keeping it alive, no thought can survive.

NIGHT

Imagine that you're looking into a great big magnifying mirror. Every wrinkle, every pore, every imperfection is blown up so gigantically that you appear—in your own mind—hideous. Grotesque. You simply cannot stand yourself.

You have company in this experience.

If you could see the thought bubbles over the heads of people as they walk down the street or wait in their cars at the traffic light, you would become conscious of all the self-flagellating, self-loathing language floating like particles of dust in the air. *I'm a loser. Pathetic. Ugly. Fat. Stupid.*

We believe this to be the truth of who we are.

But then you might encounter someone so totally luminous that those thought bubbles are nowhere to be found. They are immune. Protected. Love lives in them so profoundly that there is no room for anything else.

You know these people. Maybe you're already one of them. At ease in your own skin. No longer shaken by the collective insanity and noise that continually distract you from your own magnificence. No longer internalizing the voices that have demeaned you or denigrated you. *No longer believing the lie.*

The Divine wants you to know that you are beautiful.

You are perfectly formed.

You are enough.

When you begin to make room for this acceptance to flower within you, it will grow and grow until you cannot imagine it being any other way. You will be held so completely that you are shielded from judgment in all its forms. This shield is not anything like armor. It isn't external. It isn't harsh. It is as soft and fluid as a sea of light.

In this sea of vibrational fluidity, the words and opinions of others will flow right through you. Those thought bubbles—your own, and those of others—have no place to stick. In this sea, there is no possibility that any kind of judgment can latch onto you. Relax and witness this flow. As your eyes gently close, as you pull your blanket up to your chin, feel yourself so full of love and light that it is simply impossible to be touched by anything else. There is light all around you. Bathe in it. Know that it's there.

Feel it filling you from head to toe. Luminosity. When you wake up tomorrow morning, notice that you are less encumbered by the burden of judgment. You are buoyant. Light. Fully present. You are a gift to yourself and to the world around you.

Day 7 Patterns

Have you ever stood at the bottom of one of those old city buildings that has, at its center, a spiral staircase that goes all the way from the lobby up to the top floor?

Well, those buildings look a lot like our lives. With each step we climb, we gain greater and greater perspective. But buildings have a finite number of steps and floors. In the case of life, *the staircase is infinite*. The staircase never ends.

When we discover a pattern, a repetitive cycle in our lives, our first impulse is to try to break it. But our patterns are there for a reason. They're meant to teach us something important. Eventually, what we really want is to get to a place of appreciating our patterns—because regardless of how we perceive it in the moment, everything that happens in our life is a catalyst for change and growth. When you feel as if you've tripped and fallen on the same exact step over and over again—whether that step is financial turmoil, or heartbreak, or disappointment, or lust—you are, in fact, on a *new and different step, on a higher flight of stairs, each and every time.*

With every breath, you are making your way up that infinite staircase. With each step, we are able to recognize and appreciate that we are never passing through the same moment twice. So within a few breaths of where you fell over, you are already fresh and new. You're constantly in a new place of awareness and experience.

You'll never meet the same step twice.

We have common themes and patterns that show up in our lives. Marrying the wrong guy, losing and gaining the same ten pounds, being able to meet only the minimum payment on your credit cards. We will meet these common themes and patterns in a more evolved way in the fullness of time. The oppression of your twenties is the liberation of your seventies. At seventy, you have greater perspective. You're further up the staircase. So even if you're still tripping and falling, it means something completely different than it did when you were younger.

Project yourself, for a moment, into the future. Look back—as if through the opposite end of a telescope—on yourself as you are right here, right at this moment. Perhaps you're sitting on a sofa with your feet up, reading this book. Perhaps you're riding the commuter train. Maybe your kids are small and crawling underfoot, or they're off at college, or you don't have kids. Maybe you're worried about the size of your bank account, or what you're having for dinner, or whether you should become a vegetarian. Maybe you just had the same fight with your spouse for the hundredth time. Look back at yourself from further up the staircase. Sometimes viewing our lives from an expanded perspective can be enough to break the pattern. What do you see? Does whatever it is that you're tripping on today still matter? Of course, we know from experience that it doesn't. This is the gift of perspective and awareness.

NOON

The patterns that make up our daily lives can become ruts. We fall asleep on the same side of the bed each night. We take the same route to work each morning. We catch the same train. We sit in the same car. Talk to the same people. We use our favorite mug for our tea. We make our kids the same breakfast. We answer the phone in the same manner. Habits. These are ingrained so deeply within us that we don't even notice or recognize their repetition.

Of course, these are minor examples. Many of us comfortably live our whole lives this predictable way. But then there are the subtle patterns that can be more problematic and harder to recognize. Perhaps you find yourself drawn to emotionally unavailable people, but then you wonder why, when your beloved uncle passes away, none of your friends offer to accompany you to the funeral. Or, in romantic relationships, maybe you've chosen cheaters again and again, but still you fall for a new guy whose marriage recently broke up because of his affair.

This is unconscious choosing.

We have the opportunity to become aware of and alive to our own motivations. Our own unconscious choices. When this happens, we can begin to *choose differently.*

More courageously.

More lovingly.

From a place of freedom.

When our patterns are revealed to us, we face a fork in the road. Are we going to take the road less traveled? Or the one we've worn down with our ceaseless, fruitless pacing?

When I was growing up, my uncle would always say to me, "Don't be a robot." I was seven years old, and I had no idea what he meant, but his words stayed with me. As I got older, I realized that people—grown-ups—often live the same day over and over again. Years pass. And nothing alters. This kind of robotic repetition can seem like safety—but when I see people living inside their patterns, it's as if they aren't quite alive. Their need for stability is suffocating them. Their light is diminished. Their patterns have become a web, strangling them.

A friend of mine who grew up in a suburb of New York City once told me that her parents had friends who had never been to the city. Can you imagine? One of the world's greatest metropolises in their own backyard, and they were too paralyzed by fear and insecurity, by lack of curiosity. They had succumbed to the very robotic existence of which my uncle spoke.

So here is today's challenge. This afternoon, instead of eating lunch in front of your computer or while working at your desk, pause for a moment. Break a small habit. See if perhaps that lets a bit of air in, as if you were opening a window and feeling the breeze. If you always eat alone at your desk, instead—if the weather is temperate—invite a colleague to join you on a park bench or in a nearby café. Think about how this change in routine affects your day.

From here, expand your thinking about what your deeper patterns are. If you tend to avoid eye contact with a particular senior colleague, make a point—just for today—of saying hello. If you never do anything spontaneous, surprise your wife with a small gift or tickets to a play. Notice the way that altering the small stuff leads to thinking about the bigger picture.

After all, if you don't climb out of your unconscious rut—if you don't allow yourself to take risks—you will never truly know what blessings life has in store for you.

NIGHT

We measure our lives in minutes, hours, days, weeks, months, years. We are babies, children, teenagers, young adults, middle-aged, elderly. But time as we understand it does not, in fact, exist. Time is a mental construct. *The dimension of energy and spirit is timeless.* We are living our lives all at once. And because of this, we are able, at any given moment, to access all that we are. We are able to tap into our higher selves. To access greater connectivity. Greater love.

Imagine that you are on the top step of the very long and very beautiful spiral staircase I mentioned earlier. If you look over the railing, you will see it unfurling below you, floor after floor after floor. From this vantage point, you are able to see every indentation, every place where you might possibly trip and fall. The shining banister. The iron balustrades. Over your head there is an ornate skylight made of beautiful stained glass. And above the skylight, infinity.

If we could always see our lives through the eyes of our highest self, we would understand that this spiral staircase is our journey and that what may appear to be our own limited pattern is actually a part of a much greater pattern. From this place of seeing, we can look at our progression. We can observe it all—our whole lives—as it unfolds.

From this top step, we can guide ourselves.

We can teach ourselves to trust the fall.

We are meant to trip and fall. Every trip and fall is leading us to a greater vibrational threshold. If we could see the blessing, we wouldn't be so afraid.

Trust the pattern. This pattern is yours—as individual as a snowflake. In this pattern is every lesson you need to learn. Every reason you've been born into this body, this moment. This pattern *is* you.

From the top of the spiral staircase—from your highest self—reach out a hand to your younger self, the one who is reading this book at this very moment. Your higher self is telling you that it's okay—all of it. You are in constant motion, ever spiraling upward. Yes, you will trip and fall—but never on the same stair, never in the same way. As you drift off to sleep, look down at yourself with love and compassion. See yourself for the beautiful, perfectly imperfect, exquisite being that you are. Understand that *your patterns are your journey*. They are the musical score to the great adventure of your life.

DAY 8 Addiction

MORNING

Shine the light of awareness on addiction, and we see it for what it truly is: *distraction*. Anything that distracts us from what is happening right now is an addiction. Addiction can also be seen as avoidance. In our culture, the definition of addiction is so loaded—drugs, alcohol, sex, gambling—but actually almost anything can be an addiction. In order to tackle addiction, we need to restate it. The word itself is too huge and has too much stigma and weight and severity around it. How can you, of your own volition, even begin to navigate that reality? Sugar, caffeine, exercise, social media, Internet shopping, the phone, email, obsessive housecleaning, you name it—if we understand and rephrase these as *distractions*, then we bring it all into the context of either being present for life or not.

If you're experiencing the wholeness and completeness of life, you are allowing yourself to feel the underlying energy. We're afraid, or sad, depressed, or grieving, or furious, or envious, or even joyful, and we reach for the industrial-sized bag of M&M's or the bottle of vodka in the freezer, or we click on Net-a-Porter to see for the twentieth time whether those Prada boots have gone on sale yet. When we do this, we are avoiding our feelings. And we've learned by now that when we avoid our feelings, what happens?

That's right. Vibrational density is what happens. Stasis. Nothing can flow.

But when we allow ourselves to feel the underlying energies instead of resorting to addictive, distracting behavior, the very fuel that drives those addictive behaviors starts to evaporate. In the absence of the fuel, the behavior can no longer exist. It's like trying to keep a kerosene lamp lit but without the kerosene.

What are you addicted to? A good way to get to the bottom of this is by considering how you avoid feeling. Sit down now and make a list. Don't edit yourself or question yourself. Take the charge out of this whole idea of addiction. You don't have to be drinking a half bottle of whiskey a day to be an addict. Who knows—maybe you're addicted to self-help books! Rest quietly with this new awareness of the ways in which you distract yourself. You will likely be surprised by what you discover. Awareness is the first step in breaking the cycle.

NOON

If you're reading this book, some significant part of you longs to be conscious. Otherwise, you wouldn't be waking up each morning and devoting yourself to the deep exploration of your fear, sadness, anger, guilt, shame, self-judgment, and patterns.

If you didn't want to feel, you wouldn't be here.

However . . .

A world full of feelings often seems impossible to bear. The sheer weight of that emotional burden can be overwhelming. Think of a time in your life when you've been enraged. Or profoundly sad. Or deeply, powerfully joyful.

Hard to take, isn't it?

We move away from feeling fully, because we're afraid that we will utterly fall apart.

So we're in a conundrum, yes? On some level, we yearn for feeling. But we've constructed habits, embedded them in our daily lives, to ensure that we will keep from becoming consumed by our emotions.

The day in front of you will hold challenges, large and small. Every day does. You could lose your job. Your kid could flunk out of school. Your spouse could be having an affair. Someone close to you could pass away. All these things are possible—though not likely. What is more likely is that your day will be full of small moments. Tiny adjustments. Minor indignities. Disappointments. Bits of humor. Loving exchanges. Annoying people. (There are always annoying people!)

What do you do in the face of life unfurling?

Do you open your eyes? Do you feel with your whole heart? Do you allow it all in—every bit of it?

Or do you resort to your tried and true default button?

The cigarette break.

The gossipy phone call.

Surfing the Internet.

Raiding the fridge.

I am hoping that, just for today, you'll be willing to take a leap with me. *These are all addictions.* Most of them won't kill you—though of course some of them will. But they are leeching the life out of you nonetheless.

Just for today, allow life to impact you without ducking, without scrambling for that default button. If someone irritates you, feel the irritation. If someone hurts you, be sad. If joy bubbles up from within you, breathe into it. *In this way, we cultivate emotional intelligence.*

Find the courage to feel—without distraction, without impediment. *You don't have to run away.* You may want to run from the things that will sting you, the sharp edges that might be uncomfortable—but in so doing, you're also running away from a treasure chest heaped with glittering jewels. You're running away from life itself.

NIGHT

It begins and ends with an ache. But what is the injury that has caused the ache? What has wounded us? After all, we don't ache without reason. The ache causes us to reach out. To grab. To consume. To numb ourselves in whatever ways we possibly can. The ache won't let us stop until it is satisfied. The three vodkas. The prescription painkillers. The pint of Ben & Jerry's. The bong, the rolled-up hundred-dollar bill, the needle. The self-inflicted vomiting. The Internet porn.

Or perhaps your addictions are more mundane. Perhaps they even look healthy, from a distance: the hours spent at spin class, the slavery to the scale, the perfect house without so much as a pillow out of place.

What's really happening when we feel the ache? What is it that we truly want?

The booze, drugs, dieting, perfectionism—none of it actually gives us pleasure. It may give us something that *masquerades as pleasure* for a brief moment. But this pleasure is veiled and hollow. There is no fulfillment in it. No meaning. No luminosity. No joy. No love.

This ache is loneliness. This ache is boredom. It is the sadness we cannot shake. The anger we're trying to hide. The fear that grips us in our solitude. The insecurity, anxiety, and stress tightly wound into a ball lodged in our solar plexus that demands release. We crave something authentic. And yet we reach for the opposite: a Band-Aid, a balm.

What would happen if instead we simply sat and felt the ache? What would happen if we stopped running? No one has ever died of this ache. You are not alone. We all feel it. We all know. The ache is like a knock at the door. We look through the peephole and don't recognize the stranger waiting on the other side. We're frightened. What will happen if we open the door, if we let the stranger in? What we don't realize is this: The stranger is not a stranger. *The stranger is us.* The stranger is a part that we have shunned, cast off. The part we need to embrace in order to once again make ourselves whole.

Consider the ache as an awakening.

The ache is the precursor to the fulfillment you are seeking.

It is time to explore these cast-off parts. To embrace the ache. As you lie still in the quiet of your room, relax your body. Really relax. Scan yourself for areas of tension and let them go. Now bring your awareness to your breath. Extend the breath down to the base of your spine. Feel it residing there. Spacious. Expansive. As you inhale and exhale, allow the breath to move up and down your spine. As it flows, greet the guest who wants your attention. Make room for whatever comes. Welcome it. The ache—the unwanted visitor—is actually a friend who has come to turn on the lights.

DAY 9 The Ego

If addiction is distraction, egoic existence is the biggest distraction of them all, because our egos distract us from the greatest truth there is: *We're all part of one entity, one expression.* Seemingly, ego allows us the illusion of separateness—but in fact we need this illusion of separateness in order to really enjoy the pleasures of being human, because we have to have one polarity in order to experience the other.

What if the ego is your friend? Your ally? What if it allows you to paint with the vibrant hues of Rothko, to make your guitar sing like Eric Clapton's, to navigate this vibrational plane of existence with brilliance?

The key to understanding the ego and making it your friend is the realization that everything that happens is the greater glory of the expression of the Divine coming through you. For instance, I am aware that none of this—my teaching, my appearances, this very book you are holding in your hands—is about me. I'm only the instrument through which it is happening. So I cannot take credit for it. I understand who the captain of my ship is. I understand that the infinite being who created me is using even my ego to serve its glorification.

But talking about the ego is a bit like handling sand. It's an ever-changing thing that you can't grab ahold of. The harder you try, the more it slips through your fingers. It also has the uncanny ability to fill the shape of any container—and, as we all know, it can be mighty irritating when left unchecked in the wrong place and can lead to severe chafing. So let's give it its own texture and hue, and let's actually try to feel the ego for what it is, so that we can address it.

Envision your ego. What color is it? How does it make you feel? What does it look like? Does it have a voice? Does that voice whisper or shout? Are you in danger of believing your own hype? Is it frightening? Is it manic and raw? Or is it more subtle? Does it have a sinister presence? Does it quietly lurk in the background of your experience? Here is what it might look like if you are able to illuminate and embrace it: *It will become transparent.* It will no longer skew your view of reality. It will no longer impede your ability to see the luminous nature of all things. It will be like peeling back the curtains on a bright, sunny day.

It will be your friend.

NOON

Watch yourself carefully today. Keep an eye out to see if you do any of the following: brag, lie, name-drop, interrupt, assert, dominate, compare, manipulate, insult, lack curiosity.

If you find that any of these less-than-stellar traits have crept into your behavior, you will know that your ego is running amok.

As you read the "Morning" passage, none of this had happened yet. Your day hadn't gotten under way. The world had not touched you. Nothing and no one had intruded to challenge your sense of self. But as you begin to navigate your day, you will be challenged. Your ego will be threatened. Someone will insult you or degrade you, and you will want to compensate by puffing yourself up. Your sense of self will be bruised, and you'll want to lash out. You'll want to react in an almost animalistic way, as if to defend yourself in the jungle of life.

But what do we accomplish by puffing ourselves up, really? Does it make us feel any better? Does it make us look better in the eyes of the other person?

You know the answer.

Consider the possibility that your ego can be your best friend—but only when *you meet yourself with true clarity and awareness.*

For today, take note of every single time you feel the urge to inflate, to assert, to make yourself better than—

and *stop*. Do nothing. Sit with the feeling of simplicity and the grace of being yourself. Nothing more, nothing less. No need to make yourself bigger—which, in fact, has the paradoxical effect of making you smaller. No need to posture. *Just simply be.*

When your ego is in alignment, it becomes your trusted ally with which to move forward.

As you move through this day—through the thicket of moments that could call your ego into action—instead be profoundly honest with yourself. Operate from the highest place of integrity and congruence. Notice: *I'm doing this to impress someone else. Or to make someone envious. Or to make myself better.* Seeing it is the first step toward stopping it. You won't be able to stomach it in yourself. You will notice the difference—and you will be amazed at how much better it feels to reside fully in your own simple, unadorned, radiant self.

NIGHT

What you don't know is that I am your salvation. Without me, you are nothing. You think you're supposed to rid yourself of me. I've been given a bum rap—you've been told that I am to blame for everything wrong in your life, but in fact you need me. I am here for you. I am your own small army that you can marshal at any time to help you to grow. To excel. To reach your full, radiant potential.

I am your ego.

Without me, you'd have no expression. No outlet. No distinguishing characteristics. Without me, you'd be faceless, nameless, off drooling in some anonymous corner. I am your ally. Your advocate. *I am the tool through which you are able to deliver the light you are into this world.*

I am the one who allows you to pick up the phone and ask your boss for a raise. I am there when you muster the courage to ask someone out on a date. I help you get down on your knee to propose to your beloved. I am with you when you go on your college interview. Or stand up to a friend who has hurt your feelings. Or get up to deliver a toast in front of a crowd. Someone tells you you're never going to amount to anything, and I kick in. *Oh, yeah? I'll show you. Watch this!*

I am a raw power that can, when harnessed for the good, do anything. But you haven't learned to tap into me yet. You don't need to tame me or whip me into spiritual submission. No. My challenge to you is to *accept and own who you are.* In that journey, I am your best ally.

As you get ready to sleep, align yourself with me. When you close your eyes, imagine that you are surrounded by me, as if I were a translucent force field—which, in a way, I am. Embrace my potential. Know that you are unique. That you are magnificent. That you are full of infinite possibility. Once you have fully accepted me, you will be able to use me in order to make ever greater contributions to the world around you. Ask me into your heart. Invite me in. I belong inside you as much as anything else. Soften into the feeling of limitlessness. Drift off to sleep. When you awake, when your feet hit the floor, it will be with a potent combination of power and peace.

DAY 10 I'm Not Good Enough

MORNING

One of the most powerful mantras in the English language is: *I'm not good enough.* Here's why: *because it's not true.* And yet on some level we believe it to be true. As we saw with shame, transformation, at its essence, is bringing that which remains hidden into awareness. It's like taking a flashlight, shining it into a dark corner of a room where you thought a ghost or a demon lurked, and discovering that nothing is there.

What we are able to illuminate disappears.

What we're doing is shining a light on this uncon-scious conversation. It's as if you have to walk through the wardrobe and dive into Narnia to find it. So what we want to do here is uncover your unconscious conversation, the one you have in your head in a looping, ongoing tape even when you're not aware of it. People are often unaware of this tape—oblivious to the fact that it even exists—and yet it is robbing us of life. I uncovered it only through a very in-depth exploration of myself. When I first started this journey, I got to a point where I could start to unravel myself. It was like pulling a single strand of yarn and everything else attached to it unspooled and fell away. And what I discovered were three sentences, and the sentences are:

I'm not good enough.
I'm unworthy.
I'm unlovable.

I realized that these thoughts were my constant companions. They accompanied me everywhere I went. Even though I felt very connected to the Divine, it wasn't as if that connection granted me immunity from the highs and lows of everyday life. What I found was that these unconscious conversations run through the tapestry of every single human being. They're part of an energetic field that exists on this planet until collectively we break through it. It's dangerous for anyone to assume that they're immune from these conversations. The connection to the Divine allowed me to *see* all these subtle layers that most people don't have access to—but it didn't protect me from them. Little by little, once I became aware of these conversations, I began to embrace them. To chant them. And I came to realize—like Dorothy, the Lion, the Scarecrow, and the Tin Man walking the Yellow Brick Road—that these thoughts weren't real.

Put down this book and sit quietly. Close the door.

Give yourself three minutes. In only three minutes, this exercise is transformative.

I'm not good enough.

I'm unworthy.

I'm unlovable.

Say this out loud, again and again. You may feel resistance. Sadness may emerge. Do it anyway. Don't stop.

I'm not good enough.

I'm unworthy.

I'm unlovable.

In my workshops, I have seen profound responses to this exercise again and again. A successful businessman in his sixties sits on the floor, repeating *I'm unworthy* perhaps a thousand times, sobbing—sobbing deep, ugly sobs because, underneath all the trappings of his success, in the secret, dark recesses of his inner life he believes himself to be unworthy. A young woman in her twenties, stuck in a pattern of destructive relationships, hunches over in her chair, repeating *I'm unlovable* as hot tears stream down her face. And do you know what happens after all those tears? After hearing those words, over and over?

The absurdity of this kind of self-loathing becomes crystal clear. And in the space that is made, self-love is born.

A note to the reader: If you do this exercise in its entirety, I will not be held responsible for what happens once the pendulum swings. Spontaneous outbursts of laughter, a deep sense of serenity, joy, and bliss may well occur. If you pee yourself laughing—you're on your own.

NOON

During the course of your day, the smallest thing can set these phrases off: *I'm not good enough. I'm unworthy. I'm unlovable.* And once we're off, it's as if a drop of dye has been released into clear, previously unpolluted water. Suddenly it stains everything. It colors our whole worldview.

Here's what happens to me when one of these phrases becomes—even for a moment—my reality. My shoulders hunch forward. My head drops. My eyes are cast downward. I assume a position of defeat, of giving up.

Even though these thoughts aren't true, they can cause a physical reaction—one of contraction, withdrawal—and that physical reaction then negatively impacts reality. A vicious cycle begins. I think, therefore I am.

When we are in a posture of receiving, we can feel ourselves open fully. We become larger, expansive. Have you ever had the experience of thinking someone is much taller than she is—because you've imagined her as tall? This would be a person whose energy, whose way of navigating the world, comes from openness, and that very openness expands her physical being. But when we are governed by the nasty little thoughts that serve to undermine us and keep us from our full potential, *we shrink*. We shrivel. We are like a half-inflated balloon.

And we are doing this to ourselves.

Have you ever watched as a game is lost by a golf pro?

Or a tennis champion?

Or a star quarterback?

You can see it in them—the moment that a switch is triggered and their consciousness becomes mired in a self-fulfilling, losing prophecy. *I'm not good enough.* They lose a point, then keep losing. They assume the posture of defeat. Defeat begets defeat.

You can see it in a championship boxing match. Or in the slump of a kid's shoulders in the midst of a difficult homework assignment. Or in the sabotaging of a relationship. *I'm unworthy. I'm unlovable.*

The moment you give up on yourself, you've cut yourself off. *When you give up on you, there's nothing outside you that can help.*

But you can learn to catch yourself.

Just for today, use your body as your guide. So often we are disconnected from our bodies, but if we truly listen, we receive a wealth of information about what's actually going on within us. Notice your body language. Are you curled up? Arms crossed? Fists clenched? Jaw tight? Are you skulking? Are you marching down the street like an automaton? Are you fidgety, bouncing your leg up and down, drumming your fingers?

Notice.

Follow your physical reactions today almost as if they're a trail of bread crumbs through the forest that allows you to see what's really happening. Recognize those damaging words playing out in your head, affecting your life. Once you see those words for the lies they are, you will be taking an important step in the direction of your true and beautiful nature.

You are good enough.

You are worthy.

You are loved.

NIGHT

You accidentally knocked over a glass of red wine on a first date. You were about to shoot the winning basket for the team, and you missed. You stuck your foot in your mouth, inadvertently insulting a friend. You messed up the family recipe on Thanksgiving.

It's the silly things. The silly things that make us think we're not good enough. This subtle energy is like tar—stretchy, sticky. There is no escaping it. There's something wrong with us—we're sure of it. We did something. Or didn't do something. Said something. Or didn't say something. We make mistake after mistake, causing us to come to the conclusion that we are unworthy.

We try ourselves in our own court of law and find ourselves guilty. We pound the gavel. We sentence ourselves to lack. To suffering. To scarcity. To a minor, low-key, ongoing desolation. All because of this endless list of silly things: the spilled wine, the missed basket. We may not even remember our inner laundry list, but it resides somewhere within us. It lives in our bellies. In vulnerable moments, just when we think we might actually be worthy of success, happiness, contentment, joy, the gavel slams down.

Not good enough.

These small indignities peck at us. They sting us like a swarm of pesky mosquitoes, biting, causing welts. We itch and itch. And eventually this itch creates density. There is only one way to dissipate this energy: Acknowledge that it's there. It's a part of you—but it is not all of you. You are not solely the person who spilled a glass of red wine on a first date, even though in your mind you have become a klutz who never does anything right. You are not simply the player who caused his team to lose, but in your mind you have morphed into a total loser who single-handedly brought defeat to his school.

Take in these self-definitions. Feel them. *Be unworthy.* As you lie in bed holding this book, feel that sense of complete and total unworthiness. The spilled wine. The missed basket. The bad dinner. The wrong words. Whatever your accumulation of silly things happens to be, feel it. Feel it all. Lie there wallowing in it. Feel it rolling all around you.

After a few minutes, you'll notice something happening. All that unworthiness is a whole lot less interesting. Maybe it's even a little boring. That which we allow ourselves to fully feel eventually loses our fascination. The charge fades and fades, like a battery running out. It's dead now. All those silly things. All that wasted energy on being not good enough. It's done.

And now, as you drift off to sleep, notice how much more interesting it is to count sheep or to let your mind wander over the details of your day without settling on all the things you did wrong. You've released yourself from this petty unworthiness. You've earned your rest.

Sleep tight.

Day 11 Shattering Inner Sabotage

MORNING

Once you begin to embrace your own worthiness, you will also begin to encounter ways in which you undermine it. As long as you believe those three unconscious sentences in that constant loop through your mind, you are sabotaging yourself. You're so filled with judgment and self-criticism that you can't possibly receive your innate abundance, your innate joy and wisdom. Think about how you feel when you receive a compliment. *You look beautiful today. What a wonderful dress. That was a terrific speech. You have such a nice house.* Do you take it in? Do you receive it with grace, acceptance, pleasure, joy? Or is there something inside you that rebels against it? That inwardly pushes it away? That, to put it quite simply, *just doesn't believe it?*

The Divine is a loving friend who is always trying to bring us everything that we need. But because we're so filled with feelings of unworthiness, we're never fully able to receive this nurturing bountiful presence in our lives. We can be in the most magnificent place in the world but unable to appreciate it if we are not fully at ease with ourselves.

How often do we see people reaching the pinnacle of success only to blow up their lives? They have everything they could possibly want in a material sense, but still they're miserable. This is because they haven't addressed their unlovability, their feelings of being not good enough.

We resolve our inner sabotage by dispelling the false evidence, so that we can see the truth of what life is. Realize that *life is unfolding for you.* For most people, this is a leap. What does this mean? Surely it doesn't mean that life is—for all of us, or any of us—some perfect, rosy path. As our lives unfold for us, we are able to see that even the most painful and traumatic experiences allow us to be of greater service. This happens not through the avoidance of the human condition but rather through being available for *every single facet of what it is to be human.* I've had to have my heart broken in order to be able to be there for someone whose heart is broken. I've had to feel the depths of my loneliness in order to meet others in theirs. I've needed to experience my own happiness in order to meet another person's happiness with joy rather than envy. Life's experiences, regardless of how they show up, are *the means through which we get to love one another.* This needs to become the governing principle of your reality.

The universe unfolds and unfolds. If we cultivate an

awareness of this, our inner saboteur is destroyed by a fundamental trust in the greater pattern of things, which is born—or, better yet, *remembered*—in our hearts. This doesn't mean that everything is always rosy. We all know better than that. But when we open ourselves to the spaciousness, the vastness of experience and energy throughout time, we begin to sense this unfolding. Even the most unthinkable of losses—I am recalling a woman I know who lost her young daughter to a sudden raging infection—can, in time, lead to unforeseen beauty. Many years later, that woman adopted a baby from China—not a replacement for her beloved daughter, of course, but here life unfolded *for her*. There was magnificence glittering in the midst of devastation.

None of us are immune to the subtle and not-so-subtle voices of inner sabotage. We need to keep ourselves on a maintenance plan, just like brushing and flossing our teeth. Course-correcting the inner saboteur is a lifelong process. You're not going to just sit here and banish that voice in your head and never hear from it again. But you can recognize it when it emerges. Act out of a conscious awareness. If you remain present, in the fullness of all that you are, there will be no room for the saboteur. As you move through this detox, one by one you are turning all the lights on in the house of your heart. If you are reading this book, you are poised for a breakthrough. You probably wouldn't have picked it up, and you certainly wouldn't be this far into the detox, if you weren't.

So keep a careful watch out for your inner saboteur. Be vigilant. Understand that there are two times in life when it is most likely to kick in: When things are getting really good, you'd better believe that the inner saboteur is right around the corner. And the second, more insidious time is when you're about to have a breakthrough.

NOON

In the weeks after my appearance on *Super Soul Sunday* with Oprah Winfrey, I expected that I would be on top of the world. After all, I had just experienced an extraordinary series of events that I had never even remotely dared dream of. But instead of being buoyant and hopeful, I felt lonely, sad, and insecure.

This huge light had shined on me, and then, after the light was turned off, all I felt was the darkness.

I was left alone to wrestle with my inner saboteur, who had been lying in wait for precisely such an opportunity.

Here are some ways my inner saboteur went to work: I became brassy, immature, arrogant, and entitled. Acquaintances shied away from me. Who could blame them? I began to envy others. I became sad and lonely and tried to fill the void of that sadness and loneliness with food. I gained weight. I felt unhealthy. In business situations, my inner saboteur kicked in as I dictated how I thought things should go, and I came perilously close to alienating the people around me. I began to troll Twitter and Facebook for positive reinforcement from complete strangers. I stopped being available to my family. All of my time was spent either stuffing my face with food or hunching over my iPad. Look how many people retweeted me! Look how many liked my post on Facebook!

It was all sadness and loneliness. Instead of being full of myself in the best sense—which is to say, full of spirit—I was instead just full of myself. Unworthiness, self-loathing, feeling like a fraud—it all took ahold of me.

My inner saboteur had completely taken over.

Your inner saboteur is not going to kick you when you're down. It will lie in wait for the moments when life begins to unfold in new and exciting directions.

A new relationship.

A promotion.

The birth of a baby.

An unexpected windfall.

These are the moments when you need to be on high alert. Just as I was unaware that my saboteur was at work in those early days after my interview, it will not be easy to see at first.

Here is one way to know when your saboteur has taken over. The people who love you—the ones who truly want what is best for you—will try to let you know that perhaps you're not acting in your own best interests. You won't want to listen. But tuck this away for future reference. *The voice of love always has your back.* Even when you don't know it. Even when you don't want to hear it.

The voice of love—which is no different from the voice of the Divine—begins as a gentle whisper. If the whisper is not heeded, it will get louder. It will speak more forcefully until it becomes a shout. A scream. Eventually you will hear it. As you move through your day—just for today—listen carefully and catch the whispers around you.

The key is to catch it when it's still a whisper.

NIGHT

Imagine a magnificent moment. Perhaps you're at the beach with loved ones on a crystal-clear day. The sky and the ocean are the bluest of blue. Everything sparkles. The sandwiches in your picnic basket are beyond delicious. Everything and everyone surrounding you is radiant. You're reading a book you love. A flock of seagulls flies overhead. The waves lap gently at the shore. Suddenly, as if a shadow has fallen across your beach towel, you have a thought. It comes to you unbidden: *Maybe there's something terribly wrong with me. Maybe I have cancer. Maybe I'm about to have a stroke. Maybe there's a blood clot in my leg.*

Or let's say you're driving along a highway on another beautiful day. The radio is playing one of your favorite songs. You're on your way to meet your best friend for a fabulous lunch. Suddenly you picture the tractor-trailer in front of you jackknifing, causing a massive terrible accident. Or you picture a deer bounding out from the forest and careening through your front windshield. Everywhere you look, there is carnage.

You look at your perfect sleeping child in her crib and imagine that she isn't breathing. You bend over and put a hand on her chest. For a split second you are certain that she has been ripped from you.

These are the thoughts of your inner saboteur. The saboteur comes after you only when you are your happiest and most fulfilled. It is a jewel thief, lying in wait for the most flawless stone, the most precious jewel, the chest full of gold, before it comes to snatch it all away. After all, your saboteur is going to make an appearance only when there's something to sabotage. *You don't deserve this bounty*, it whispers. *I'm going to come steal it all away.*

This inner saboteur is your disrupter. It is a fear-based energy that arises in the presence of peace. Peace represents its extinction. It does whatever it can to disrupt your sense of peace, abundance, success, fulfillment so that it can continue to survive. *The inner saboteur is a creature of our own minds and making.* It is what we feel when we wait for the other shoe to drop, when we imagine doom and gloom around every corner.

But in order for the inner saboteur to bring you down, it requires your participation. It does not, in fact, exist without you. *The inner saboteur will disappear when faced with the formidable opponent of courage.*

It requires courage to face down the inner saboteur. To

say no: No, I'm choosing to be happy. Choosing to be content. To be joyful. To accept life's blessings. To feel worthy. To feel deserving. To live my life to its fullest without worrying that the other shoe is going to drop.

In the face of courage, the saboteur has no choice but to put its tail between its legs and slink away.

As you get ready to turn out the lights—to slowly slumber into possibility—embrace all that you are. Fill yourself with a sense of kindness and clarity about *all* of you. Not just the parts that are simple and easy to admire but also the parts that you perceive to be more complex, damaged, darker. It doesn't matter.

You are deserving.

You are complete.

You have everything you need in order to flourish.

Bear witness to your own breath. To the soft bed beneath you. To the earth beneath that bed.

This breath.

This earth.

Trust them. They are supporting you in every way you need. When you awaken tomorrow morning, you will do so with a renewed sense of clarity and authenticity. You will know yourself. You will be grounded in spirit. To know yourself is to know the Divine.

Day 12 Triggers

MORNING

We find ourselves hanging out with the same people. We engage in the same conversations. We go to the same restaurants or the same vacation spots. We find like-minded people and, in finding them, we think that we're being fully received.

But all along we're missing the point, which is that by surrounding ourselves with like-minded people, we're diminishing the impact that life has on us. We're narrowing the opportunity to grow and expand.

We avoid people and situations that trigger us. We consciously do this. We're afraid of that which is different. We're taught not to marry, not to befriend, not to associate with people who are of different ethnicities, religious backgrounds, political ideation, even people who have different taste in books. Oh, that person likes chick lit, and I'm partial to Jane Austen. That person is a Yankees fan, and I'm a Red Sox fan. Democrat, Republican, member of the Tea Party. Staggeringly wealthy, dead broke and homeless. Healthy or ill.

Next time you feel your buttons being pushed—and make no mistake about it, it is a physical sensation that you can feel, right in your solar plexus, if you tune in—instead of fleeing or resorting to distracting behavior, just stand there. Experience everything inside you when you're in that environment. Don't shut down. If you can stand there and feel the truth of the situation and of yourself, you will feel a tremendous surge of energetic power. Say to yourself: *I am not going to move away from this situation because it's uncomfortable.* The most uncomfortable situations in life hold the greatest potential for growth.

People spend much of their lives running away from people who trigger them—but I run toward them. I jump into environments where I'm triggered, because it's the only way to authentically dissipate these energies. Once, I was on a radio show and a gentleman called in to say he didn't believe anything I was saying. He was trying to invalidate who I was. In that moment, I was absolutely aware of my insecurity. Instead of running away from it— becoming defensive, evasive, better than—I just sat in the discomfort of this perceived attack on my credibility. I sat in the fear of it. By welcoming it, by staying absolutely in the discomfort of it, I began to be able to find a peacefulness around it, which authentically led me to being okay with whether somebody gets it or doesn't get it. It doesn't matter. Being triggered in this very public way brought me to the realization of how necessary it was for my development and my growth, for me to own who I am. I put myself into these uncomfortable situations because *I don't want there to be anywhere in the world where I am not at home.*

I'm here. I'm real. Deal with me.

NOON

Perhaps this morning dawn's light had just begun to creep beneath your bedroom curtains. Your family was asleep, your pets curled up in their respective beds. The house was silent. Gloriously quiet. And suddenly: *Brrrring! Brrrring!* Just about the worst sound, first thing in the morning. In the kitchen. The den. Your office. If you have a baby, as I do, now that baby is awake. There's crying along with the ringing. The dogs stir. Barking too.

You knew who it was going to be on the other end. Every muscle in your body tensed before you answered the phone.

Yes. You were right. It was your maniac boss. The one who doesn't sleep and has no boundaries. The one who thinks it's his right to call your home at any hour. You sat up in bed. Your wife glared at you and got up to try to soothe the baby.

It's the third time this month that your boss has pulled this stunt.

Your boss is a trigger. You know this because even though his behavior is unacceptable, you haven't found the strength to face him down. To stand up for yourself. To draw a line in the sand.

Why not?

Consider the possibility that your triggers have something to teach you about yourself. Something you need to learn.

In being triggered, you are being given an opportunity to grow. Instead of tensing up, shutting down, gritting your teeth, grinning and bearing it, what would happen if you were to simply remain open to what this trigger is telling you about yourself? In the case of your boss's call, the energies of fear, anxiety, and powerlessness are standing in the way of the action you need to take.

If you remain open, those underlying energies will not have the chance to stick with you. Instead of forming a rock in your gut, they will be like small craft on a river flowing through you. And you will have the clarity to act with equanimity and discernment.

Triggers happen. We can't avoid them. They don't always present themselves in the form of a crazy boss. We've all had the experience of meeting someone—at a business conference, or a holiday party, on the edge of a playground sandbox—and having a visceral, intense reaction to the person. We can actually feel ourselves recoiling. A friend of mine often hears a phrase running through her head at moments such as these: *Wide berth*, she thinks. *Wide berth.* As in: Steer clear.

But we can't always steer clear.

In fact, the people who trigger us are some of our best teachers.

That nasty colleague who always seems to be sneering at you and succeeds in getting under your skin: Why is she getting under your skin? What makes it feel so *personal?*

The trigger is your mirror.

The trigger is showing you something about yourself that may not be pretty or comfortable but is present nonetheless.

As you move through your day, take a second and feel it each time someone gets under your skin. What's going on? Ask yourself what feeling is being dredged up from deep within you.

What is this trigger telling you that you need to know?

NIGHT

Cast your mind across this day just now coming to an end. Cast it wide, like a net, missing nothing. Think about each moment, each experience, each person, each encounter, as best as you can recall. What do you catch in the net? Barnacles? Or pearls?

When you walk yourself through your day, surely you recall moments that felt clear and comfortable: tea with an old friend; a sweet phone call from one of your kids; a brisk walk after dinner. But then there are the other moments. The ones that don't feel so clear or comfortable. The ones you'd just as soon forget.

Instead of forgetting, focus your attention on these moments.

Perhaps your in-laws constantly make you feel like an outsider in their family. Or maybe you have the same running argument with your spouse. Or you might have a friend who is more of a frenemy—who knows exactly how to get under your skin and make you feel insecure.

These are instances of *triggers*.

Though we might wish to run away from these people or situations that trigger us, what will ultimately heal us is *running toward them*. We don't want to do this. Every fiber of our being wants to turn away. We don't want to *feel*. But triggers are present in our lives in order for us to come to a greater level of self-acceptance.

Make yourself available to the discomfort.

Open the door to experiencing whatever this person triggers in you.

That which activates you liberates you.

It shines a light on what you need to know.

You cannot get annoyed, frustrated, infuriated, made insecure, when you are at peace with yourself. It simply isn't possible. No matter how much people try to ripple the calm that you are, they cannot. You are unshakable. Beyond disturbance.

As you finish sorting through the ups and downs of your day, gather in your mind all of today's triggers. Simply the awareness of them is an excellent start. Now imagine that they are small gray stones. As you lie in bed, settling in for the night, imagine your body becoming water. You are growing wider and wider. Bigger and more expansive, until you are a deep and glorious lake. You are surrounded by mountains. No boats are allowed. You are huge, calm, completely undisturbed.

Now take those small gray stones, one at a time. Name each of the moments that triggered you. One by one, toss those stones into the vastness of you. Watch the ripples as they emanate out. The bigger you are, the smaller the ripples will be. As you fall asleep, maintain this sense of vastness. Tomorrow, when you once again find yourself triggered, come back to this place. Once again, enlarge yourself. Enlarge your heart, your soul, your spirit. And watch as the ripples diminish.

Day 13 Soulful Surrender

MORNING

I was twenty-three when I reached my breaking point, on that incredibly intense New Year's Eve. I now understand that everything had to be stripped away before any real change or transformation could happen. I now also know that this stripping away was a profound blessing.

After I shook and quaked in fear all through that night and morning, I finally reached a point at which there was nothing left to do but surrender. My terror stopped when I came to understand that everything happening to me was originating from the Divine. I began to trust in that— I felt I had no choice—even though I couldn't see the outcome. And that's the definition of trust, isn't it? To surrender without knowing what will happen. To surrender in faith. On some level, I knew that what was happening to me was an invitation from the Beloved. I was being asked to rest my head on the shoulder of the Divine. From a place deep within myself, I asked:

Please help me.
I'm tired of doing this by myself.
Whatever this is, I'm ready.

I felt a nausea, a twisting and turning in my stomach, a terrible anxiety, a sense that I was about to be swept up in something greater, and the deep, deep knowledge that as a result of that experience I would never be the same again. The feeling was somewhere between the anxiety that you feel before going on a first date and the fear and grief that you experience as you're on your deathbed, taking your last breath. There was the sweetness of that first-date anxiety—after all, I had been looking forward to this for a long time—and at the same time a profound fear and sorrow, a grief that my life as I knew it was coming to an end. That surrender led to my experiencing the Divine in its totality.

I know it isn't this way for everyone. Soulful surrender opens the doorway to receiving, *whatever that receiving might look like.* For some people, the surrender leads to a connection to God. But what it really amounts to is a moment when you simply can't manage on your own anymore. When you stop holding on to how it's supposed to be. When—literally or figuratively—you sink to you knees. You can't shoulder the burden alone.

Soulful surrender begins with two small, powerful words: *Help me.*

When you're having a hard day, when you don't know where to turn, when you're scared to death, know that there exists a safe place where all that you are is embraced. *Help me.* A place where the tenderness of who you are is completely embraced. A place where the creativity that you cannot contain within your body is housed. *Help me.* A place where the memories of anger and rage and depression become figments of the past, aspects of a former self you once knew as the truth of you.

NOON

Just for today, tread lightly. Meet every moment with gentleness, with a quiet certitude, with vulnerability. When you drive to work, instead of weaving in and out of traffic, gripping the steering wheel for dear life, listen to soothing music and breathe deeply; stay in the slow lane.

What would happen if you were to move through your day *as if you've already lived it*? If you've already lived it, then you can glide gently through each hour as it unfolds. Everything has already happened. You don't have to press. You don't have to fight. You don't have to assert yourself or your will.

You don't have to control anything.

All you need to do is be present.

I'm asking you—just for today—to surrender. Instead of rushing willy-nilly through the hours, move softly. Instead of clenching, flow gracefully. Make a conscious effort to slow down. To breathe. Each part of you is going to want to race off, like a greyhound at the track. But what I want you to do is stop. Understand that racing and rushing wastes energy. Picture yourself as a dancer. Fluid, graceful, elegant, precise.

You may have to surrender many times today. You may have to remind yourself of this way of living life *as if it has already happened.* Your mind is accustomed to operating at warp speed. The very world we all live in is designed for that warp speed and rewards it. But it takes a tremendous toll. By speeding through life, asserting your will, you are violating your own connection and harmony. Frenetic behavior breeds more frenetic behavior and serves to further disconnect you from yourself.

Connect.

Connect deeply to the wellspring within you, the wellspring that is always, always present, waiting for you to tap into it. As you move through your day, have patience with yourself. Be kind to yourself. This slowing down, this surrendering, is simple—but it isn't easy. Everything within you will want to keep you mired in the familiar.

Surrender.

Imagine if you could live your life this way—not just today but every single day.

I have news for you.

You can.

NIGHT

We tumble into bed. We stick earplugs in our ears. We take a sleeping pill. We watch our favorite television show, numbing ourselves. Or we toss and turn, agitated about what happened today or what will happen tomorrow. At times we think of sleep as our enemy—when, in fact, sleep is the best friend we know. Sleep is the ultimate act of surrender. This is where we access the deepest parts of our psyche and consciousness. The Dalai Lama has called sleep "the best meditation." This is where it all happens— where we can open ourselves to our deepest work.

So how do we make the most of this rich land of sleep?

We begin with the essential: a necessary feeling of trust.

We ask ourselves: What has our backs?

In order to trust, we must feel supported. Stop reading for a moment, and take a look around your room. Do you have everything you need to feel safe, comfortable, cosseted? When was the last time you asked yourself what you need?

The bed beneath you. Your pillow—your trusted companion. Your blanket. A glass of water on the bedside table, or a cup of steaming tea. How is the temperature? Are you too warm? Too cold? Do you want the window open? Perhaps it would be nice to have a gentle breeze, the sounds of nature surrounding you. If you don't have everything you need in order to soulfully surrender, pause for a moment. Put down this book. I'll wait. Instead of making do with what is, go find whatever it is that will make you feel fully and completely nurtured.

Okay. Are you back now? All set?

You have set the stage for surrender.

Consider this an invitation.

An invitation to give yourself over to the unknown.

An invitation to let go and surrender to a vast sense of expansiveness.

An invitation to trust the Divine.

When you were a newborn, no one had to tell you to do this. There was a time in your life when you just gave yourself over. You knew nothing different. Take yourself back to that place of innocence, to that place before fear. Before sadness. Before anger and self-judgment. A place of simple and utter surrender. By giving yourself over in this way, you are allowing yourself to receive everything that you need.

Sleep soulfully.

Sleep like a baby.

Let go.

Living In Possibility
An Exercise

As you get comfortable with this new flow of
emotions, take a moment to think of a way to start
showing up differently in your life as a result of
this Density Detox. Whether it's regarding your
health, money, relationships, or your loving connection
to spirit, how would you like to do things differently?
Write it down on a piece of paper and put it in an
envelope. Leave the envelope open, but put it in a
safe place, because we're going to come back to it.
This is only the beginning.

DAY 14 Change and More Is Coming

MORNING

It is our nature to want to hold on to the moment. We want to grab on to whatever is happening—good or bad—as if it's the branch of a tree hanging over the rapids. We reach up, trying as hard as we can to grab on to that branch, because we are afraid of the rapids beneath us. We're terrified of the current. But life is never stagnant. It flows all around us, whether we like it or not. Have you ever heard it said that you can't step into the same river twice?

We're frightened of change. We want a crystal ball. We want someone to somehow tell us how it's going to be. But all the while we're missing the point, which is that energy is ever-evolving, and change is our way of navigating our own vibrational expansion. When we become willing to let go, we align ourselves with the universal principle of more. *Change is always a good thing, regardless of what it might look like at the time.* Ultimately, it is always leading us into more. Remember: This is a law of nature. As our energy evolves, change happens. *A shift in energy is always followed by a change in reality.* Fear of change causes stress. To fear change is to deny the natural impulse of who you are.

Don't get comfortable! Change is the one thing we can count on. Look up at the sky and see that the clouds are moving. Sit under a tree. Watch the leaves gently sway in the breeze. This planet that we inhabit is ever-evolving. The sun rises and sets. The tide moves in and out. Nature demonstrates to us in each moment the principle of flow. We are provided with a constant reminder that stagnation equals density. A big step toward detoxing from the density that has been holding us back involves not only accepting change—but also welcoming it.

Let go. Holding on to the past, or trying to freeze-frame the present, only impedes your ability to receive more. And that's what this whole journey is about, after all.

Receiving.

Abundance.

The universe wants to deliver more to you. If you get quiet enough, you can almost hear it whispering: *more, more, more* . . . Be that water flowing along the riverbed. Move freely, quickly, unimpeded. Sure, there is debris along the sides, all caught up on the banks of the river. But that's not you. Feel yourself flow—gracefully, simply, without impediment. Change is a law of nature. Embrace it.

NOON

If you're like most of us, you probably woke up this morning with a predetermined idea of how your day was going to go. You had your date book full of plans: the dentist appointment, the interview, the afternoon spinning class. You checked the weather forecast. You made a dinner reservation.

And then life happened.

Take a friend of mine who recently dropped her son off at boarding school. She and her husband were pretty sure they knew how it was going to go. They'd spend the afternoon with their boy. Then, after an emotional farewell, they'd drive to a country inn, where they'd spend the night recovering from the emotional upheaval of leaving their kid at school. But what *actually* happened was a different story. The day was uneventful. The goodbye, fairly easy. Everyone was excited and happy. My friend and her husband went to the country inn, enjoyed a nice dinner, and awoke the next morning to the news that their son had fallen and broken his leg during a hike. He was on his way to the hospital for X-rays. They needed to come back to campus.

The best-laid plans.

We plan and God laughs, as they say.

Of course, we all need plans. We have our schedules, our BlackBerries, our calendars full of dates that sometimes stretch months if not years into the future. But this is understandable and useful only as *structure*. Not as the blueprint we hope and believe it to be. That blueprint is a fantasy.

Life is always changing. Every minute of every day.

So how do we navigate this awareness, this certainty of change? How, when it is human nature to want solidity and stability? We love certainty, even as we bury the knowledge, deep within us, that certainty is an illusion.

As you navigate your day, know that it isn't going to go as planned. Not exactly. Hopefully you will not have to face anything as dramatic as a child with a broken leg. But surely there will be many impromptu moments. Life is full of the unexpected. And thank goodness! Would we really want our days to play out exactly as we imagine? What fun would that be?

Just for today, as you head into the great unknown, do so with a commitment to yourself to roll with every punch. To be fluid and even spontaneous when presented with the surprises that are in store for you. Your boss gives you a difficult assignment? Excellent. Breathe into it. You get caught in a downpour without an umbrella? Okay, so you get wet. So you're going to have a bad hair day. So what? Unexpected dinner guests? Order a pizza.

The point is to lose that quality of rigidity—of density—about *the way it's supposed to be*.

In fact, see if you can strike the phrase *supposed to be*, along with *but it's not fair*, from your vocabulary.

Today is about learning a lesson in openness. In gracefulness. In acceptance. And, ultimately, it's about realizing that change always means more is coming. We can't know what these changes will be. But we can trust that expansion is the law of the universe. Just as a heavy, humid, stifling day presages a thunderstorm that will leave in its wake beautiful, clear, cooler weather, change is a part of nature. Inevitable. *It is a catalyst and a blessing.*

Just for today, let go of your version of how life is supposed to be.

NIGHT

As you lie in bed, clench every muscle in your body. Go on—clench them. Start with the arches of your feet and move up through your thighs, your belly, your fists, until you finally scrunch up your face and clench your jaw. Hold yourself this way for a couple of minutes.

Then let go.

Exhausting, isn't it?

Exhausting to try to hold on, to live with that kind of tension.

To grasp at nothing—for no reason.

The world we live in convinces us that we must struggle, that struggle is the norm. We are taught that if we try hard enough, we can control our destinies and the destinies of those we love. We amass possessions. We erect fortresses. We build up our net worth. We believe all this can protect us. We send our children to the best schools within our means—and we convince ourselves that this will en-sure their future happiness and success. We tell ourselves that we can safeguard them against struggles, so that they won't have to experience pain or sorrow. We hold on for dear life. All the while we are missing the point, which is that we are not in control.

In every single moment, *change is happening all around us*. We breathe in and out, and change is happening. We get up in the morning and go to work, and change is hap-pening. We put our children on the bus, and change is happening.

Have you ever watched a particular tree through all the seasons? The way the branches begin to redden slightly at the very beginning of spring. The way those same branches gather leaves, become green, lush in summer. Then au-tumn arrives, and those leaves turn color. They wither and fall to the ground. Eventually they are covered by snow. *Our every single moment is like that cycle of nature—only we are unaware of it.* We do not watch ourselves as if we were that tree. We imagine that we are fixed. Solid. Immutable. But as long as we are alive, we are changing.

Think of yourself a year ago. Are you the same person? Whatever the measure of time—a generation, a lifetime, a decade, a year, a day, an hour, a minute—we are evolving. We can no more stop our own evolution than the tree can stop itself from flowering.

Now, as you stretch out in bed, scan your whole body

for all the places you clenched and tightened. Imagine them being filled with spaciousness and light.

Change is coming.

Change is always coming.

There is a profound freedom in the acceptance of this. As you close your eyes and ready yourself for sleep, think of yourself as that tree. What season are you in? Are you at the beginning of spring? In the midst of summer? Are you feeling the bittersweet nostalgia of autumn? The starkness of winter? Know that whatever season rises to your mind—that, too, will continue to change and evolve. That is the one singular certainty.

Change. You can count on it.

Know that it is always leading you into more.

Day 15 On Light

MORNING

Close your eyes. You are surrounded by a brilliant golden ocean of energy. Even if you resist this—even if you're certain that you can't possibly do this meditation—try it anyway. Trust me. The feeling associated with this energy is the purest form of love you've ever felt. You can begin to touch it. To feel it. It's all around you. All you have to do is be present for it. You can begin to become excited by the possibility of living in connection with this beautiful golden light.

Take a moment and just do this before you begin your day. Before your kids start calling for you, before the emails start piling up, take this time. I promise you that anyone can do this. Yes, that means you.

Invite this brilliant golden luminosity into your toes. Then invite it into your feet. Your ankles. Your calves, shins, knees. Your thighs, your pelvis. Allow yourself to be filled with this golden light, this love. Allow it to flow up into your belly, your lower back, solar plexus, mid-back, and then up into your chest and upper back. Into your shoulders, your biceps, triceps, elbows, forearms, and then streaming down into your hands, fingers, and thumbs. This light now travels up into your neck, your throat, jaw, mouth, nose, eyes, ears, forehead, and then fills your entire head, all the way up to the crown.

Even if you're having trouble feeling this, stay with it. Give yourself this gift. What do you have to lose?

You are completely filled with luminosity, so much so that there is no longer any separation between the light and love inside you and the light and love that surrounds you in every direction.

Rest in this experience for a while. Consciously acknowledge the truth of who you are. Thank yourself for taking the time—for overcoming your own resistance—for quieting down all the voices in your head. The separation between you and the Divine ends here.

NOON

You are not alone. There is a light within you that accompanies you every step of the way. This light is a soft presence. It is a feeling, a sense of calm and protection that surrounds you. Throughout your day, this light is with you. Just for today, tune in to this knowledge that you are not alone.

Feel this light during your every waking moment.

When you're at lunch with a coworker. When you're crossing the street. In the elevator. In your car. Picking up your children. Shopping in the grocery store. Washing the dishes. This light is with you.

You will feel spacious, centered, peaceful, complete. You will witness and observe. Time will slow down.

You will feel absolute love.

You will recognize this light in others. It is the light of the Divine. Separation falls away. You will become open to listening and receiving. If you focus on this light, you will be shifting out of fear and into love. This is perhaps the most important shift any human being can undergo.

You will feel your soul and the souls of others.

Along with being aware of this light within you, notice that everyone you encounter during the course of this day is also accompanied by this light. See the goodness in everyone you meet. Catch their radiance as if it is a sunbeam.

Acknowledge kindness. Generosity. Grace. Clarity. Wisdom.

If you look for it, you will see it all around you.

See this light in your partner, in your children, in your neighbors. See it in your pets. This light exists in every living creature.

All I'm asking you to do today is to be aware of this light. If you lose it, come back to it. If you struggle, close your eyes and just simply feel. You will encounter a presence, an energy, a companion, a source. You will hold within yourself the deep knowledge that *you are not alone.*

You've never been alone.
And you will never be alone.

NIGHT

I am golden luminosity. I am your beloved. I am the one you have been longing for your entire life, whether you have been aware of it or not. I am here to love you. To fully embrace you.

You are my one perfect creation.

My opus.

When you were born, I marveled at your magnificence. We have never been separate. Never apart. Your heartbeat and mine are one and the same. I am the breath that expands your being. I am the light that animates your form. I am the love that floods your experience. I am the brilliance you display. I am the blessing that is shared through you into this world. You are an extension of me. An ambassador. Through you, I am able to love all of my creation. You are the embodiment of everything that matters to me.

I am always with you.

I was there in your mother's womb. I was there when you were born. When you uttered your first cry. Your first tears. Your first words. I was there when you learned to walk. On your first day of school. When you were bullied in the playground. When you were the teacher's pet. I was there when you fell in love for the first time. When you moved away from home. When you got your first job. Your first promotion. When you had children of your own. When you experienced grief and loss. When you made and lost friends. When you moved across the country. When your parents passed away. When you noticed the first lines etched on your face. When you pulled out your first gray hair.

I was with you for all of it.

There hasn't been a single moment of your entire life when I have not been with you.

Know this.

Know this with every part of yourself. Know that I walk alongside you, that I reside within you. There is no difference between us. *I am you.* Rest in this knowledge. Stretch out and feel the enormous comfort of this—the way a cat might stretch out on a soft rug in a perfect beam of sunlight.

Bask in it.

Bask in me.

I will watch over you as you lay sleeping.

And I will be here waiting when you awake.

Day 16 Roller Coaster

MORNING

News flash: Life is not going to stop happening. Not for an hour, not for a minute, not for a nanosecond. The more we try to control life, the more life closes around us, like one of those impossible Chinese finger puzzles—the more we struggle and try to pull our fingers out, the tighter it gets.

Just about halfway through the Density Detox, you may find that you are beginning to meet life with a new sense of grace and ease. Think of a roller coaster. Do you know how, in an amusement park, you'll see two types of people who ride the roller coaster? First there's the type who holds the railing so tightly that her knuckles turn white, her face a contorted mask of terror. And then there's her friend riding next to her—probably the one who convinced her to get on the contraption to begin with—who is shrieking with joy, palms open, high up in the air, face flushed with freedom and an almost childlike euphoria.

Choose. Which one do you want to be? How do *you* want to feel on the roller coaster of life? Do you want to spend your time on earth petrified and shut down, or do you want to have your hands open, squeezing out every bit of juice? Imagine: At the end of your life, which way would you like to have lived?

I'm not suggesting that it's going to be easy. The roller coaster is full of peaks and valleys, of course. As life continues to happen, it brings with it a myriad of feelings—fear, anger, frustration, loss, grief, as well as contentment, peace, joy, and the deepest love. The true skill when it comes to riding the roller coaster has to do with *maintaining a sense of openness to life as it's happening*, instead of trying to control the uncontrollable. How do you do this? By *allowing*. Remember, fear is an energy that we can allow to run through us.

The fear of the adventure on the roller coaster is worse than anything that might actually happen. Fear exaggerates. That's its natural tendency. But no matter how life twists and turns, no matter what the speed, if we maintain that openness, we can keep a sense of peace in the midst of it. A young woman I know was stopped at a traffic light in a tiny car—a Mini Cooper—when she was rear-ended by a city bus going fifty miles an hour. Her car was completely wrecked, and yet she opened the door and walked away with no injuries. Later, she told me that at the moment of impact, her body went limp. She just completely . . . let go. We all know what would have happened if she had tensed up. Every bone in her body would have been broken.

If we find ourselves in a state of contraction, then the fear becomes dense—it has nowhere to go. It fills us up and consumes us without our even knowing it. But we can learn to take my young friend's posture into life, into everything in life. If we're in a state of openness, the flow remains open.

Close your eyes for a moment and imagine something you're particularly neurotic about. Not the thing that terrifies you most but just your basic garden-variety phobia, fear, neurosis. It could be anything: elevators, escalators, bumblebees, airplanes. You name it. For the sake of this exercise, let's say roller coasters are your thing. Your friend has convinced you to take a ride, and so you strap yourself in. Already, your palms are damp. You feel sweaty, a little light-headed. The car starts to move up, up, up. What's that creaking sound? Does the amusement park do a good job of maintaining its rides? *Up, up, up.* Frantically, you look down at the people on the ground. What if your car comes unhinged? What will the newspaper articles say about the tragedy in the amusement park? How will your obituary read? You *knew* you should have burned your old journals. Now what if your husband reads them? *Up, up, up.* Meanwhile, your friend—the free spirit who convinced you this was a good idea—has her face turned to the sunlight. Her eyes are closed in anticipation. A smile plays at the corners of her mouth. You're at the very top now, the still point, the moment before the plunge. *Down!* The car moves faster and faster. Your entire body is a rictus of fear. Your heart feels as if it might explode. You come screeching to the end of the ride. Next to you, your friend is laughing delightedly. You are alive. In one piece. Nothing terrible has happened. Nothing—except that you missed the entire experience and allowed density to win the day.

Now, here's an idea. Take the ride again. Yes, you heard me right. So often, isn't that what we really want to do—no matter how frightened we were the first time around? We discover that there is nothing to hold on to, nothing to be afraid of. Nothing, except our own limited vision. Fasten your seat belt with a sense of joyful anticipation. *Up, up, up.* The ground recedes as you move up toward the sky. You're breathing deeply, trusting your spirit and the spirit of those around you. *Whoosh!* You fly down, the wind in your hair, your voice rising with a chorus of others. You're going along for the ride, fully engaged and alive.

NOON

If you're a control freak—and who among us isn't at least a little bit of a control freak—the hardest thing in the world is to let go. That's right: *Let go.* You want to micromanage every single aspect of your life. You think that if you don't focus on every single detail, every single nuance, your life will fall apart. But by grasping on to life this way, you're living under the illusion that you can control the universe.

Do you unnecessarily make life more difficult and complicated than it needs to be?

When you're on a roller coaster, what has you holding on for dear life? Fear. If you're a perfectionist, a control freak, what makes you want to hold on to everything and everybody around you? That's right: fear. This calls to mind two friends of mine who live in the same neighborhood. These two women are in their early forties. Both are smart, educated, attractive, and successful. Both are happily married and have a couple of kids. Their circumstances are very similar—but their outlook on life could not be more different. When one friend calls me to chat, she sounds buoyant, happy, grateful for her life's gifts. She's full of stories about her children's accomplishments, her husband's latest project, her own triumphs at work. When my other friend calls, however, she begins with a litany of complaints. She's always stuck behind the wheel of a car, schlepping her kids from one playdate to another. Her husband is a slob. Her career is in a slump. She feels old, and tired, and put upon by life. *These two women's circumstances are interchangeable*. The difference between them is that my first friend looks at her life through the lens of love and the other through the lens of fear.

We are either in love or in fear.

We are focused either on what we have or on what's missing.

We either embrace experience or shut down experience.

From the time we're born, we're on a roller coaster; it is the shape of life itself, with its ups and downs, its curves, its peaks and valleys, its slow climbs and breakneck plunges. *The ones who enjoy the ride are the ones who let go.*

This requires cultivating a state of wonder.

Think of the way a young child can spend many minutes contemplating a single flower. Or that same child's fascination and delight over juice spilled on the floor. Somewhere along the way, as we grow up, we lose that sense of astonishment. Of delight and pleasure. We lose the ability to sit back and watch life unfold as if it were the greatest movie ever made.

As we mature, we become aware of the roller coaster. We become aware of its perceived dangers, the stomach-lurching sheer drops. We begin to live in anticipation of these rather than in appreciation for what's right in front of us.

Just for today, dig deep for that childlike sense of wonder. It's still inside you. You only need to look. Begin by appreciating whatever is around you at this very moment. Your glass of orange juice. The ant creeping across your kitchen table. The beam of sunlight pooling on the floor.

The vine of ivy and the graceful twists it makes along your windowsill. *Whatever you see, appreciate it.* Be curious. Take it in as if for the first time. Now, as you proceed with your day, take this sense of wonder with you wherever you go. The toll collector. What's his life all about? The tunnel you drive through on your way to work. What was it like to build that tunnel? Imagine it! How utterly amazing!

Instead of getting all caught up in the minuscule world inside your head, step outside, onto the roller coaster of life. Just for today, enjoy the ride.

NIGHT

In all likelihood, in your house right now there are multiple electronic devices whirring, beeping, and ringing. More and more information is adding up: chores, responsibilities, things to do, places to be. Even checking your in-box can feel like a ride on a roller coaster. We live in a chaotic, chronic state of high alert.

What has been lost in the translation?

We have.

We've lost ourselves.

We've forgotten how to *be*—and everything that goes along with that simple state of being. Curiosity. Wonder. The blessing of being bored. The simple joy of staring out the window, allowing the imagination to run wild—with all the gifts that imagining can bring.

We've sacrificed our internal connection. Sure, we're more "connected" than ever before—but we're paying a price, and that price is the roller coaster.

The antidote to all this noise and busyness—this roller coaster of life—does not require effort. In fact, it requires the opposite of effort. It requires a complete and total relinquishing. This is not about the illusion of control anymore. We know we're not in control. We're beyond that. Now what is required is to *simply allow*.

Allowing does not require doing.

It is *non-doing*.

It is being available to whatever is.

When you allow, all sorts of space opens up. Space in your consciousness. Space in your heart. Space in all five of your senses. Because you are not fighting, not struggling, not resisting, suddenly there is a lot more room.

What do you usually do when you finish reading this book for the night and prepare for sleep? Do you quickly take a sip of water, then turn out the light? Do you *will* yourself to sleep?

Tonight, try this: When you finish reading, put this book down next to you on the bed. Don't turn out the light yet. Just be. Look around your room. Consider this a meditation. What do you see? What do you hear in the rest of the house? Floorboards creaking? Leaves rustling against the windowpane? Rain pounding against your roof? The sound of a shower running downstairs? What do you smell? A whiff of laundry detergent on your sheets?

Garlic still permeating the air from the eggplant parmigiana you cooked for dinner? Can you taste the residue of toothpaste in your mouth? Can you feel the cotton of your pajamas, soft against your skin?

Can you do all this simply by allowing it?

Not thinking about it?

Not judging it?

Not ascribing a value of any sort to it?

Let us simply bear witness to what is. Through the simple act of allowing, we are deeply connecting with that which makes us human.

Okay. Now turn out the light. You are drifting off to a place beyond language. There is no struggle here. No fight. Nothing to resist. Sleep hard. Sleep well. Sleep is the ultimate act of allowing.

Day 17 Tracking Our Thoughts

MORNING

If our thoughts created our reality, we'd all be in very big trouble. Just imagine if your every thought became real. *I hate myself and wish I were dead. I hate this other person and wish she were dead. I'm a hideous person and deserve the terrible things that happen to me. I think I have cancer. I don't have enough money to pay the bills.* Whatever your particular inner tape is, it loops around and around, doesn't it? Trying to stop thinking is like trying to get Niagara Falls to stop being a waterfall. But *thoughts aren't the enemy.* They just float on by. We're like cowboys out in the wild, and we think we have to lasso our thoughts—harness them—as if they have intrinsic power. But the truth is that our thoughts—without being backed up by emotion—have no power. They have no juice. Only when a thought is consistently accompanied by a feeling does it yield any control over your life.

It's actually our vibrational density—the way emotions

become stuck in our system—that gives our thoughts power. In the absence of that density, our thoughts would be like beautiful fluffy clouds that drift by. There's a prevailing idea out there that we should try to shift our thoughts, to forcibly change the content of our minds. But that isn't possible. Just give it a try. Right now try to change your thoughts in a specific area. Say, if you're preoccupied with a matter at work or a fight you had this morning with your husband: Try not to think about that.

How's it going?

That's what I thought.

It doesn't work. And now, on top of your self-perceived failure for not being able to change what you think about, you're also beating yourself up for thinking things that you shouldn't be thinking. You become your own thought police. Instead of doing that, let's start *untangling our thoughts from the underlying emotions that hold them in place and give them meaning*, why don't we? That's true freedom, right there.

Think of your thoughts as an invitation to open Pandora's box.

Begin with a thought you have all the time. For instance, one guy I work with finds that his thoughts constantly veer toward a place where he's comparing himself to other people. Is he up? Is he down? Is so-and-so's career going better? Does so-and-so have a hotter girlfriend, more money? Every thought this guy has somehow leads back to this place of comparison.

This comparing drives him crazy—he's well aware of it—but he can't seem to stop the looping tape. That's because he hasn't dug deeper, hasn't really sifted through his own particular Pandora's box. What's lurking beneath that rambling inner narrative? What is the deeper hidden voice saying? The endless comparisons are a byproduct of something. But what?

This fellow began to see, when he opened the box, that lurking in the muddy depths beneath every thought about comparison was a seething, powerful insecurity. He felt that he wasn't enough, that he constantly had to measure up to other people or he might just disappear altogether. And beneath that worry that he might disappear?

You've probably guessed it by now.

Fear. Fear of the unknown. Fear of insignificance. Fear of obliteration. Abject, profound fear was at the root of the stories and their endless loop.

Our thoughts create patterns—those patterns become sticky—and when something's sticky, we can't get rid of it. And so we need to ask: What's the underlying energy? *Thoughts aren't an enemy. They're an invitation.* They're like owls flying by us with notes in their beaks. We avoid these owls. We're distracted. We're looking elsewhere. We don't even see these beautiful winged messengers flying by—much less stop and carefully, lovingly remove the notes they carry.

As you get in the habit of unlocking these patterns, you

start to feel what's beneath them. And then you begin to come to a level of awareness of why you latch onto them.

The more you become aware of the energy beneath the thought, the sooner you arrive at a deeper place of peacefulness. This is the profound difference between attaching meaning to something and simply observing it.

NOON

Your day may be full of chores, meetings, items to cross off your list. A day that will contain many responsibilities. You may be taking care of your children or your elderly parents—or both. You may be running a company and have lots of people relying on you. You may be an emergency room nurse or a high school teacher. No matter what the precise circumstances, your day is probably already full to the brimming point before you even walk out the door.

So how are you supposed to track your thoughts? How are you supposed to even be aware of thinking?

You're so busy doing, doing, doing.

Running from appointment to appointment.

Supervising. Negotiating. Responding. Reacting.

Who has time to notice her own thoughts? And, anyway, why is it important? Why do we even need to track our thoughts? If we're not aware of them, do they still matter?

Oh, yes. They matter.

They matter a lot.

Because our daily thoughts are forming a pattern. This pattern—once we recognize it—is the entry point for us to access *the feelings beneath the thoughts. And the density beneath those feelings.*

When we track our thoughts, we're able to get to the underlying emotion beneath them. And when we do this, we've cracked an all-important code. Our thoughts may seem meaningless, disjointed, disconnected, just like random numbers on the dial of a safe. Fifty-four may seem unrelated to seven, which may seem unrelated to twenty-four. But when we undo the locking mechanism, when we open the safe, we discover that which needs to be resolved. And on the other side of that is everything we've ever wanted.

Your thoughts are your clues.

Observe them.

Of course, this isn't something you can do all day long. It would impede your ability to function. This is why it's so important for us to have time to ourselves, to do yoga, to meditate, to sit quietly, to journal—whatever your method is for slowing down enough to see the contents of your mind.

Just for today, I'm going to ask you to do something seemingly very simple. During the course of your day, give yourself the gift of three ten-minute increments. Decide when these increments will take place, so that you don't get swept up in your responsibilities and miss them.

During these ten-minute breaks, do nothing other than observe your mind. Silently watch your thoughts. You mind will rebel. It will go all over the place. It will want to think about dinner. It will tell you that you're hungry or bored.

Sit there anyway.

This is how you begin to rein in the mind.

Breathe and observe what's actually going on.

As you build these brief moments into your day—as you pay close attention to the contents of your mind—you will begin to come home to your true nature. This is freedom! By recognizing your unconscious patterns, you will be empowered in a whole new way.

NIGHT

Did you lock the door? Did you take out the trash? Uh-oh. Did you leave any candles burning downstairs? What about the fireplace? Are the embers safe to be left for the night? Is the oven turned off? Have you walked the dogs? Is the cat inside? There are coyotes out there, after all. It's eleven o'clock in the evening. Do you know where your children are?

If you were to track your thoughts before you drift off to sleep, they would tell quite a story along these lines.

They would be an aria of worry. A symphony of niggling doubts. Background noise. An endless list of what-ifs. We all have these what-ifs. They actually serve a function, these looping thoughts that are part of our decompression at the end of a long day. They are harmless—as long as they don't start sticking together, thereby creating density within us. We don't have to be debilitated by these thought patterns that appear when we first rest a head on the pillow. We need to understand them for the transition that they are.

Otherwise, we are in danger of making mountains out of molehills. The small anxiety about whether or not you've taken the garbage out can quickly escalate into a terrible fear about that new super virus, which you just heard about on the news, and the world coming to an end. The niggling concern about whether the cat is indoors (you *know* the cat is indoors!) can escalate into paranoia about mass murder or nuclear devastation. The mundane can suddenly turn fantastical and catastrophic. And then—*boom!*—you are wide awake. It all feels incredibly real. Your heart races with every terrible thought your mind can muster.

Understand that this mundane background music—the cat, the garbage, the back door—is a buffer zone, separating day from night. We don't have to be jolted out of our serenity—and so it's important to understand that, though the thoughts come, we do not need to act upon them. *They are phantoms of our own making*.

We dismantle these thoughts first by witnessing them. We recognize them as a recurring pattern. *Oh, hello, old friend. Here you are again.* Notice that you experience the same cluster of thoughts again and again. This is not a new movie playing out in your head.

Allow this pattern to recede to a murmur.

That's all it really is.

You have every right to this moment.

To this peace and quiet.

To this space and tranquility.

You have done everything you need to do, and now it's time to just *be*. The door is locked. The oven is off. The candles have been snuffed out. The dog is in his bed. The cat is downstairs purring. Your children are reading their own books under their covers.

All is well.

All is well.

All is well.

DAY 18 Harmony

MORNING

I once had a profound encounter with a monk. I asked him to explain to me the middle path of harmony and balance as demonstrated by the Buddha. I'd been hearing a lot about it. What was this middle path all about? It seemed awfully narrow. It seemed very easy to fall off. I asked the monk: "How do you stay on the path?" And this was the monk's response: "Panache, *make the middle path so big that you can never fall off.*"

I thought, *What the bloody hell is he talking about?* But after contemplating it for a while, I realized: Our spirit is all-inclusive, so the more inclusive you are, the bigger your path becomes. Eventually, like the Buddha, it is possible to become inclusive of all things. And once we become inclusive of all things, we have complete freedom and harmony.

Harmony is our natural state. We return to harmony by lovingly beginning to dismantle any and all discord.

We embrace everything and everyone *as it is*. Love—the purest form of it—is all-inclusive. If you truly love someone, you don't just love a few of her finest qualities. No. You love her every brand of crazy. That's how the Divine loves. When I experienced the Divine, what I felt was precisely this all-inclusive love. The Divine simply embraced me as I was.

All of my crazy.

All of me.

We need to lovingly embrace life as it is. And make the middle path so all-inclusive, so wide, that you cannot fall off it.

Think about it: You sit down with a girlfriend for dinner. She's someone you love but, to be honest, she drives you a little bit nuts. She says something to the waiter that you think is condescending. She tells you a story you don't particularly feel like listening to—perhaps you've heard it before. She has a habit of humming under her breath. And you sit there and judge. You are having a lovely dinner on the surface, but beneath the surface you are in disharmony. If you are sitting in judgment, you are maintaining the illusion of separateness. Judgment and harmony cannot exist in the same place.

When I begin to feel annoyance rising in my body, I take the posture of experiencing. I relax. I'm open and available to it. I allow the energy to be present in my body. I observe it without judging. The judgment would lead to it dominating whatever else is going on. My middle path might include anger, irritation, and creativity, all at once. My middle path is wide enough so that no one feeling takes over. We need to accept and allow our emotions so they don't cripple us and prevent us from navigating life because we're so caught up in them. There's room for it all. We only need to witness.

NOON

Harmony. Even the word itself is beautiful, isn't it? Harmony is what happens when we meet life openheartedly. When we meet life from our soul.

Our soul abides in a constant state of peace.

When we live soulfully, we cannot help but be in harmony. It's only when we're coming from the limiting confines of our own identity—this body, this career, this bank account, this relationship—that we experience discord and chaos.

Just for today, expand yourself. Become so inclusive in your daily life that you embrace everything that *is*. Incline yourself in a direction in which you notice your inner dialogue. Is it leading you to a place of distance and separateness or toward integration and harmony? And don't beat yourself up about whatever you find. Just notice. Notice when you're moving away from love and when you're moving in the direction of love. Because to be in harmony is to love.

Move beyond the outlines of your own body. Allow yourself to become bigger. Give yourself a broader context for this day ahead of you. Remember that golden light from a few days ago? Surround yourself with that same golden light. It will accompany you, envelop you, make you see that you are so much larger than you think. From within this state of grace, allow your light—the one within you—to flow into this ocean of light that is all around you.

Recognize that it is one and the same.

You, the light.

There is no difference. No separation.

Here is a revolutionary idea: *You don't have to try.* This isn't about beating your head against a wall. This isn't about forcing yourself. Quite the opposite. Just soften. Use the breath. Feel yourself in your body. Listen to the ambient noise of your reality. Become aware of the smells surrounding you. *Really see.* Look outward rather than inward. All of this will ground you in the experience of the present moment.

Soften, soften.

Try not to take anything personally.

For the whole day.

What's happening is happening.

Moment to moment, put this into practice. You will begin to feel a spaciousness around you—cushiony, enormous, and at the same time impermeable. When you abide in this soulful state, you are profoundly protected from any vibrational density. It simply isn't possible. Your soul is working through you.

Don't be surprised if you feel slightly euphoric. This feeling—arrived at naturally—is what many people reach for in the form of drugs or booze. But in those cases they're trying to check out, whereas here you are opting in. You're all in. You are meeting life with openness, with softness, with vulnerability. With love.

Say to yourself: *I am in harmony with all that is real.*

No judgments. No worries. No predictions. No plans. Just this.

Spend this day unfurling into love.

NIGHT

Do you love yourself—all the different parts? Or only the ones you think are acceptable? Are there parts of yourself that you're still holding back? What are you afraid of? Do you feel that even your nearest and dearest would shun you if they knew certain things about you?

Maybe you're not perfect.

Maybe your story isn't so pretty or shiny or easy to understand.

We all have our inner crazy.

Every single one of us.

If we were able to turn ourselves inside out and show our seams to one another, we would see that—though the details might be different—our inward selves are remarkably similar. Still, we hide parts—even from ourselves. Call it shame, fear, sadness, anxiety, guilt. *Whatever we are motivated to hide keeps us from discovering our inner harmony.*

You will know this harmony when you feel it.

It is like nothing else.

You will become peaceful, contented, accepting.

You will feel an appreciation for all that is.

When you are able to embrace yourself fully, you will be infused with a sense of ease. No more fighting with yourself. No more tug-of-war about what's acceptable and what's not. There will no longer be any need to assert yourself or to retreat. In the absence of the endless internal conflict that we visit upon ourselves—the comparing, the concerns about not being good enough or successful enough or that so-and-so has more, ad infinitum—there will suddenly be space in our minds. And into this space floods every higher aspect of our true nature. We become more evolved. More involved. More curious. More empathic. We become better teachers and better students. We have an instant and indelible connection to the world around us—a world that, when we're stuck in our self-conscious little dramas—we hardly even notice.

So let me ask you again.

Do you love yourself? All of you?

Drop your sword. Stop the endless fight against yourself. There is nothing to be gained from this fight. The most powerful expression you can offer the universe is surrender. The most powerful way you can thank the Divine is surrender.

So surrender.

Name those supposedly shameful qualities silently to yourself.

Right now.

You know what they are.

Instead of trying to separate yourself from those qualities, embrace them. They are a part of you, just like every other part. You would not be you without them. You would not be loved without them. They are as much a part of you as sinew, muscle, and bone.

Surrender into harmony. As you fall asleep, know that your sword no longer serves you. There is nothing left to slay. And when you awaken, prepare to experience the world anew.

Day 19 Ever-Present Truth

So many of us place our magnificence in the future. Or leave it behind in the past. We suffer now for dreams of later—or dreams gone by—instead of recognizing that *magnificence is accessible only in each moment.* It's so simple, really, but it's one of the most difficult ideas for us human beings to grasp. All we need to do is to learn to follow the breath. All we need to do is to Be Here Now. The ever-present truth of life can be accessed *only* in the present moment.

That should be pretty simple, right?

Well, it turns out, not so simple.

Sometimes when I think of ever-present truth, I imagine a convening of the gods on Mount Olympus. A conference of sorts, where the gods—you know, Aries, Aphrodite, Zeus, the whole lot of them—were trying to decide where to place man's magnificence. (I picture them sitting around a giant conference table drinking their café lattes—but that's another story.) Let's call it the Conference on Magnificence. The gods agreed that our own magnificence had to be in a place where we would be able to find it but not without searching. And so the gods were really getting into it—they're gods, after all, and they were over-caffeinated—and then one of them came up with a brilliant idea.

"I know—let's place it right under their noses. They'll never look there."

"They'll go to sacred sites."

"Yeah, and on pilgrimages."

"They'll read books."

"They'll look to other people."

"But in the simplicity of each breath, it's occurring right under their noses!"

"Brilliant. Our work here is done."

This breathing business doesn't have to be super complicated or weird. We don't need to breathe through alternate nostrils, or retain the breath, or follow a specific rhythmic pattern, or do sharp exhalations. We don't need to sit in lotus position with our eyes closed. We don't have to be surrounded by candles or incense or be in complete silence. The breath brings us into the present. In Sanskrit, the word *prana* is a verb, an active word that means "to fill with air, life, wind." The yogic practice of this is called *pranayama*—the witnessing of the breath. In the Hebrew language, a word for "spirit"—*ruach*—also means "wind." The breath is spirit. The breath is energy. And it is literally right beneath our noses. It is in witnessing the breath that we come fully into the present moment and discover our magnificence.

Once we are aware of this, we enter the possibility of *making our lives a living meditation*. Meditation cannot simply be compartmentalized, placed into a little box where we go and sit for five minutes a day, or twenty, or two hours. *Breath and spirit are your constant companions*. What if you lived in this awareness all the time? Would you ever accumulate any density?

No. It would be impossible.

Vibrational density and a full, abiding attention to the breath cannot coexist in the same body.

So be aware of your breath when you awake in the morning. As you plant your feet on the floor to begin your day. As you brush your teeth, wash your face, pat eye cream beneath your eyes. Follow the breath as you make the coffee, feed the dogs, pack the lunch boxes. As you see your kids off on the school bus. As you dress for work. As you ride the train. Follow the breath as you interact with coworkers. As you have lunch with your difficult boss. As you answer emails. Stay in touch with the breath and notice how the world grows larger all around you, and your own sense of spaciousness along with it.

These days, I change diapers. I take out the trash. I clean out the kitty litter. I wash dishes. I feed babies. Basic mundane things. I don't wish away a single moment and find myself projected into the future. Nor do I float on a wave of memories or regrets or even nostalgia about the past. This early parenting—my wife, Jan, and I are parents to twin baby girls—is the ultimate practice in being in the present moment. As the Carly Simon lyric goes, ". . . stay right here, 'cause these are the good old days." That's true for all of us. Every single moment we live will become those good old days eventually. So wouldn't it be a good idea to be present for them?

I have yet to meet a human being who is talented enough to breathe in the past.

Nor will I ever meet a human being gifted enough to breathe in the future.

All we can ever breathe in is the here and now.

Magnificence, in each moment, is what resides within you.

Magnificence is not a destination.

NOON

We've established by now just how difficult it can be to stay present in the moment. It seems as if it should be simple, but ultimately it's one of the greatest challenges of being human. We know that *love is the ever-present truth*. But this knowledge doesn't always translate into action. It is immensely difficult to abide in that place of love in an ongoing way.

We get pulled out for a million and one reasons.

We get ticked off at a friend. We're frustrated at work.

We experience anxiety about one of our kids. We worry about our financial future. We flee the present and become consumed by the future, the past, the what-ifs. And once we've been pulled out, it's so hard to go back in again.

We need to develop tools.

Today's practice contains within it one of the best tools I know for entering that place of ever-present truth.

Right now, I hope, you're sitting in a comfortable chair. You're alone in a place where you can remain for a few moments, undisturbed. Be sure this time is just for you. Turn off your cell phone. Close the door.

We are going to expand your energy beyond your body.

Close your eyes and take some deep breaths.

Relax your body. Your palms are open.

Within you resides a pristine pink light.

This is the light of love.

With your eyes closed, locate this pink light within your heart. Now feel this light expand. It slowly fills your body. Feel it moving all the way down to your toes. All the way up to the crown of your head. Bask in this light.

Once you're completely filled with this pink light, feel it expanding beyond the confines of your body. It moves softly around you, like a vaporous cloud, overflowing in all directions until it fills the entire room.

This light moves beyond your room and fills your house. It floats into every corner and crevice. From the floorboards to the roof, from the basement to the attic, this pink light is everywhere.

Now this beautiful soft pink light fills your town. Your city. It envelops every living creature. It moves and moves, expanding until it fills your state, your country. From where you sit in your chair, in your room, you are expanding this light out into the world.

Envision our whole planet filled with the light of the Divine.

This light floats up and up—it moves into the solar system, the galaxy, the entire universe. *The ever-present truth of love reaches into infinity.*

As you move through your day, you will lose this feeling. It's inevitable. But when you do, just close your eyes for a moment and find the pink light once more.

The more you practice—the more you use this tool—the more accessible this light will be. But make no mistake. Even when you're unaware, even when you've gotten all caught up in the ups and downs of your day, it is always there. Ever-present. Waiting for you to return.

NIGHT

Do you remember a couple of days ago, when you took in everything in the room around you? Do you remember the drapes, the clock, your sheets and pillow? The creaks of the floorboards, the rustling of leaves against the windowpane? The sound of a shower running downstairs? Remember that sense of aliveness and connectedness that you felt when there was nothing left to do but to see and feel and smell and taste and touch? When you became a beating heart, at one with your surroundings?

That was a moment of magnificence.

This magnificence has nothing to do with scaling mountaintops, flying across oceans, eating in five-star restaurants, or sending your child to an Ivy League university. This magnificence is not a goal, an achievement, or a destination. But make no mistake about it: *It is magnificence.*

When we are able to completely reside in the present moment, we have transcended time and the body. We are acutely and fully alive. We are available for the present—always surrounding us but to which we are so often blinded. We're too busy for the present. We'll get back to the present later. Maybe after we've scaled a mountaintop or two. Or sent our kid to Harvard.

The sadness of this, of course, is that by rushing through our days we are missing the miraculous seconds, minutes, and hours. We are missing our lives.

Consider this an exhortation—more powerful than a simple invitation—a plea from the Divine to slow down.

Somewhere in your room right now there is probably a clock. Maybe it ticks. Maybe it's digital. Maybe it's on your television. Wherever it is, the minutes pass. Look at your clock. Watch an entire minute go by. Don't do anything else. Sit still and feel that minute.

It's taking forever, isn't it?

The seconds start to feel like hours. When we slow down, an amazing thing happens. *Time slows down too.* Where are you going? What are you doing? What's the rush? What's so important? What do you think will happen if you get there faster? Or if you stop—just stop—and be at one with the world around you?

As you fall asleep tonight, notice how many times your mind starts to careen into the future. It will do that. That's what the mind tends to do. But instead of following it all the way to tomorrow, next year, or the next century, stop and bring it back to the present. Do this as many times as you need to. You are gently training your mind in the direction of magnificence. In the same way as you would stake a plant so that it might grow in the direction of sunlight, you are staking your mind so that it might grow to embrace and embody the truth that is the present.

Fall asleep like this.

Tumble into magnificence.

Day 20 Authentic Transparency

MORNING

How honest are we with ourselves? Do we tell ourselves the truth about our experience, about what we really want and need? How we really feel? We must learn to be profoundly honest, to tell ourselves the truth instead of responding from a place of social conformity or insecurity or lack of self-awareness.

Authentic transparency is the essence of *to thine own self be true*. So often, we walk around lying to ourselves. We don't do this consciously. We don't even realize we're doing it. We fall into patterns. We go to the party, even though we don't want to. We agree to a dinner, or a date, with someone who makes us uncomfortable. We are aching to speak up—but we don't. We're afraid to be rude, or we worry that people won't like us. Or we've simply gotten used to living in a constricted state. In twelve-step parlance, we do the same things over and over again, expecting different results.

Authentic transparency is not about being transparent to other people. It is, in fact, about being transparent to *yourself.* We've gotten to know our fear, sadness, anger, guilt, and shame. We've begun to take baby steps toward loving all of these aspects of ourselves, just as the Divine loves us. Consider this: If we were honest with ourselves, how much easier would life become?

During my teens I was rebelling and trying to find my sense of self outside myself—and that wasn't working so well at all. This played itself out most dramatically in my relationship with my father. At one point, I was in New York and my dad was in London. I called to wish him Happy Father's Day and I suddenly began to cry. I had no idea it was going to happen until it did. It was as if a dam had burst. I told my dad how sorry I was, how I would never have purposely hurt him by rebelling, by rejecting him. And after a long pause, my father gently said, "Panache, I have only ever played the role you asked me to play for you. No apology necessary."

That was a profound moment in my evolution. I had found the courage—so suddenly that it felt like a shock—to articulate my feelings and my internal state. And my honesty, in turn, allowed my father the space to embrace me. It was a complete embrace. There wasn't an ounce of judgment in it, or rancor, or disappointment. He understood that I'd had to go through something—let's call it rebellion—and that it had nothing to do with him. It was a pure and simple moment.

That event led me to the realization that everyone in my life—everyone I encounter—is playing the role I need them to play for me. We all do this. If we have anger, you can be sure we will encounter someone who will piss us off. If we're sad, we will come across a person who will set off our sorrow. Ultimately, what these encounters do is to provide us with opportunities to feel *whatever it is that is unresolved within ourselves.*

Once we have felt everything that is unresolved within ourselves on a vibrational level, we then discover that these people no longer need to play their particular role in our lives. Our relationships, whatever they may be, shift absolutely. When I let go of my rebellion, my young man's rage, my need to tear myself away from my father, he ceased to be the man who I had been rebelling against, and we were able to meet in a space of pure love. Today, that same man comes to my house at ten each morning and takes care of my twin daughters, playing with them and giving them the greatest gift of all: his attention and love.

Make the commitment to be honest with yourself about what you're feeling. Fully own it. The funny part is that the very second you have this awareness, it automatically shifts your reality. You begin to see that, in becoming authentically transparent, your relationship to yourself and to everyone around you changes completely, and—I promise you—for the better.

NOON

Some days you feel as if you're living in *The Twilight Zone*. From the minute you open your eyes, the minute you utter your first words, somehow you're being misunderstood. You don't even understand yourself! You wish you could just go back to bed and start all over again—a do-over, as the kids say. But you can't. Your day has begun.

You have a few choices. You can soldier on, continuing to misunderstand and be misunderstood. You can shut down and try not to do any harm to anyone else or to yourself. Or you can take the only mindful and wise path out of the chaos: You can try to get clear about what's at the root of your momentary inner turmoil and *take a step toward authentic transparency*.

When you are in a state of authentic transparency, it's a huge relief. You will feel coherent and light. Even though things may be happening all around you that are chaotic or overwhelming, you will remain clear and steadfast in the midst of it all. You become congruent with your feelings—*because you know them*. You're not being led around by your feelings as if you're a dog on a leash.

I recently had a day where authentic transparency was an issue. I awoke to the news that my mother's car had been flooded with several inches of water during a torrential storm. For whatever reason—I wasn't in touch with reasons at this point—this news completely threw me. My household was in an uproar. I felt overwhelmed, blindsided, and ill-equipped to handle this small crisis. While in this state, I decided to drive to town to run an errand. It had been raining for days in Florida, and the ground was soaked through, muddy. In the nontransparent state I was in—unaware that I was agitated—I thought it would be a good idea to drive around a truck that was parked in an alley. And what happened? My own car got stuck in the muddy grass. Perfect! It's rare that life hands you a literal metaphor, but there it was: Me. Stuck in the mud. Wheels spinning.

This is just one story about what happens when we act out of alignment with our feelings. I was *fleeing my feelings rather than sitting with them.*

We do this so often.

We flail and react rather than go deep.

Rather than seeing what's really going on.

In my case, the truth of what was happening—the reason for my being overwhelmed—was that I felt protective of my mom. I felt that the flooding of her car was somehow my fault, that I had failed her. And this threw me back into an *old vibrational pattern.* Once I understood this, I was able to return to a state of authentic transparency. I was able to deal with what actually needed to be done.

On any given day, we go in and out of the ability to know and understand *what is driving us.* We lose our bearings, and we find them again. As you begin your day— right at this very moment—check in and see where you are. Have you been skimming over this chapter? Are you,

perhaps, impatient? Speed-reading? Maybe you're reading this while you're on a bike at the gym?

Or are you getting centered? Quiet? Taking the necessary time to be nourished by whatever you need to walk
into your day in a clear, emotionally transparent way?

Take a moment and see where you might be spinning
your wheels.

Where you might be stuck in the mud.

Authentic transparency—as its name implies—is very,
very clear. It isn't subtle. If you recognize that you're stuck
in the mud, in that wheel-spinning place, stop and get
quiet. Go deep inside yourself. Because that instant of
awareness is a sign that you're ready to turn yourself
around.

Just for today, recognize whether you're moving
toward or away from a state of authentic transparency.
Wherever you find yourself during the course of this
day—in a meeting, with your family, on your commute—
you can tune in.

You will know.

NIGHT

Imagine a house that has been shuttered for several seasons. The family has been away. Sheets cover the furniture. The shades are drawn. Mail is piled up on the front
porch.

You have the key to this house.

Walk past all the mail and packages and put the key in the lock. A spider has made her home in an intricate web above the screen door. As you enter the house, notice that dust is everywhere. Raise the shades. Fling open the windows.

As you start airing the place out, you notice cobwebs. Dust bunnies blow across the floor. The house has been that abandoned. That much in disrepair. There is grit beneath the sofa. The smell is musty. Holding your breath, you pull the sheets off the sofa and chairs. The beams of sunlight pouring through the windows illuminate the dust motes.

You find a broom and a dustpan and slowly, serenely, you begin to rid the house of all that accumulated dirt. You start to remove everything the passage of time has placed here.

Imagine this house is you.

There are places inside you that you've neglected. Abandoned. Dirty corners. Smudges of fingerprints on walls. Layers of lint and dust in places you haven't wanted to look. Here is your opportunity to clean house. To become authentically transparent. To return yourself to the original beauty and luster that is your birthright.

There is no part of you that deserves to be neglected or abandoned. No part that should be hidden from your own view.

Know yourself.

Know every single nook and cranny.

Know the spiderwebs and the dust motes, the dark

corridors, the rusted hinges. Know your sadness, your guilt, your secret desire, your shame, your grandiosity, your anger. Just as in the imaginary house, as you begin to delicately dust, you uncover the intricacy of the banister, the inlaid pattern of wood on the floor. The chandeliers sparkle, catching light. So, too, do all of these aspects of you—every last one of them—deserve to be witnessed and understood as beautiful. They, too, are a part of you. The richness and possibilities that become available when you fully embrace all aspects of yourself are beyond measure. Beneath this dust are treasures you haven't yet dared to imagine.

Day 21 Gratitude

MORNING

Here's a radical idea. What would happen if you were grateful for absolutely everything? And by everything I don't mean the great stuff or the good stuff—but all the stuff. Imagine the power of that. I often tell people that sadness is a miracle. They don't quite know how to hear this. They ask me: *How can you say that sadness is a miracle?* Well, you can—because when we trace sadness all the way back to its core, we find the Divine.

Either everything is divine or nothing is. And if everything is divine, if everything is of God, then the only thing we can do is be grateful for whatever comes. Gratitude itself has a softening quality. The Latin root of the word *gratitude—gratus—*means "pleasing." When we feel gratitude, we feel better—no matter what it is we're grateful for. Thank you for this toothache. For this migraine. For this traffic jam. Imagine it!

To be perfectly clear, this isn't the woo-woo version of

149

gratitude. It's not rote affirmation in any way. It's gratitude as an appreciation of life. If we are feeling, then we are alive. So let's appreciate what we're feeling, no matter what it might be. Have you ever stopped to ponder the idea that maybe Planet Earth is the only place in the universe where sadness—or insecurity, or grief, or rage—can be felt? What if this is the only place and time that it's possible to feel this panoply of emotion? Shouldn't we go ahead and feel whatever there is—the whole smorgasbord?

Cultivating gratitude for all things isn't so much a feeling as a decision. It is *a lens through which we choose to see the world.* Why not decide to be grateful for all things? This is the road to true emotional intelligence. Not only do we become willing to feel whatever there is to feel without judgment or rancor, but, in fact, we also throw out a welcome mat. *Come in, come in, grief, despair, loss, boredom. Come in, and make yourself at home. Anger, frustration, gripes, pull up a chair! Consider yourself most honored guests. You are a part of me, and you have so much to teach me. You are welcome here.*

If you think of life as a feast, then know that the Divine has cooked up an incredible meal for you. This meal contains amazing spices and flavors: Sweet and sour. Savory, bitter, bland. Appreciate every morsel along the way. This feast includes it all. *I'm tired. I'm annoyed. I'm in physical pain.* Delight in all of it. *I'm joyful. I'm hungry. I'm filled with happiness.* If you appreciate every morsel, imagine what your life will be at the end of the meal.

If we are authentically transparent, authentically seeing what's happening within us, then this process paves the way for gratitude for all of these states, whatever they may be. Cultivate an appreciation for the experience of life regardless of what it is. As you go forth in your day—whether you're at the dentist's office, or cleaning a dog stain off the rug, or skiing down a mountain—get your gratitude on. In so doing, you are appreciating life itself.

NOON

The Divine does not ask for our thanks. We are filled with breath, with life force. We walk amidst the beauty of this planet. We experience an incredible range of emotion. We are the beneficiaries of grace. And never is so much as a *thank-you* required.

Even though the Divine doesn't need our thanks, what opens our hearts is the very act of appreciation. Imagine if we could live in a constant state of appreciation for *all that is*?

What is unfolding around you at this very moment?

What do you see in front of you?

Everything within your field of vision is the gift of life.

Sometimes I simply think to myself: *I'm alive! Wow! I'm alive, breathing, living. It may not all be going exactly as I wish, but I'm alive! I have a family. We may not always get along, but I have a family! I have a cat! Maybe the cat scratches up the furniture, but look at this cat! It's a muggy, rainy day, but look at the gorgeousness of the raindrops streaming against my window! The lushness of my gardens!*

This is an appreciation of the mystery of the Divine. An embrace of the intangible. After all, *saying thank you for the obvious is easy.* But being openhearted to absolutely everything leads to an uncovering of unexpected sweetness, a childlike, beautiful sense of joy. Cultivate this sense of appreciation and you will find yourself moved and inspired. You will be filled with the sense that there is *more.*

Just for today, see if you can *appreciate everything you encounter.*

Stop.

Look.

Listen.

As when you walk through a museum to look at great works of art—Jeff Koons's balloon animals come to mind—there is a tremendous difference between rushing by and really stopping and taking it in. At first, the mind doesn't know what to do with Koons's balloon animals. What's this? But stopping to appreciate places you in *an openhearted resonance with that which is being observed.* When you take time to actually *be* with something, you resonate with it.

An exchange of energy happens.

But when you whiz by, you can't receive.

Your heart is shut.

You're not open to more.

Cultivation of appreciation can also transform even our most tumultuous relationships. If we could simply appreciate our spouse, our boss, our children, our friends, how transformative would that be? If we don't appreciate them, they become invisible to us. We lose our connection, our relatedness.

But when we are in this state of appreciation, *we access love*.

Just for today, observe your life as if it were a piece of precious art. Ooh and aah over every nuance, every brushstroke, each color. Enjoy the details—even if, at first, you don't understand them. Enjoy the imperfect, the uncomfortable, the strange, along with the elegant, the warm, the funny, the sweet and kind. Appreciate all of this as the extraordinary gift of what it means to be alive.

Appreciate. Appreciate, and you will begin to see every miracle and blessing. You won't want to live any other way.

NIGHT

What if we were to bless *absolutely everything*? After all, we choose our lens with which to see the world, so why not choose gratitude? What if *thank you* were to become the backbeat of every single moment in our lives? Not only for the obvious pleasures but also for the sorrows and setbacks.

It's time once again to think back on your day. What can be learned from what happened, but, more important, what can be learned from your *response* to what happened? Did you find yourself angry? Clenching? Judging? Hostile? Made insecure? Striving? Did someone cut you off in traffic? *Thank you.* Maybe your boss excluded you from an important meeting? *Thank you.* Your best friend forgot your birthday? *Thank you.*

Deliver yourself to the softness that is sometimes difficult to find in our daily lives. Instead of responding with the harsh and useless feelings that so often surround us, meet each of the moments of your day—no matter how difficult—with gratitude. With spaciousness. With the idea that every encounter, every misstep, every second of our day contains something that serves a purpose. Something for which we can be grateful, even if we don't yet know what that might be.

Gratitude is transformative. It softens us and softens the world around us. When we bless a situation—instead of judging and repelling it—we feel an instant melting. A plush, velvety softness. A nurturing presence that we will want to cultivate, once we've experienced it.

As you think back over the circumstances of your day—your tough day at work, your child's report card, your bounced check, the great movie, a surprise visit from a friend—run through each of them with this sense of softness, openness, and nurturing toward yourself and others. What does this feel like? Pretty lovely, isn't it?

As you get ready for sleep, instead of counting sheep, count blessings. Start by blessing each and every person sleeping beneath your roof. Extend the blessing to your pets. Emanate outward to all the people in your neighborhood. The butcher. The dry cleaner. The teachers at school. Every circumstance that drifts through your mind—bless it. Radiate this blessing in a circle that widens and widens until it surrounds everything and everyone as far as it can reach.

Understand that you are the center of this blessing.

You are this blessing, and this blessing is you.

You are gratitude itself.

Day 22 List of Gripes

MORNING

Gripes are a passive-aggressive way of dealing with life. A gripe isn't as powerful or pronounced as being pissed off. It's more subtle than that—and therefore slightly harder to identify. How do we express the energy of a gripe? It has a different vibe about it than the energy of anger or rage. In order to really see our gripes in full flower, we need to become aware of our own passive-aggressive nature. It's nothing to be ashamed of, nothing to feel badly about. We're human—and we all have it in us. But when we bring our gripes into the light of awareness, that's the beginning of the end of them.

Gripes are born of victimhood. Victims gripe. That's what they do. Victims also gossip. It's an under-the-radar thing, and you may not even be conscious of doing it. For example, at work, you'll gripe. Your boss has done something that bothers you—or, let's be honest, maybe you're just jealous because your boss is your boss—and you'll find ways to undermine him behind his back. You'll gossip about him with a coworker. Or you'll roll your eyes when he walks by. You'll never muster up the nerve to actually tell your boss how you feel. No. This energy is a behind-the-back thing. When we're in the energy of victimhood, we do this all the time—to colleagues, other parents at school, a doctor who doesn't treat us respectfully—really, to whomever, whatever, whenever. And let me ask you a question: What are the benefits?

There aren't any.

It's easier if you tell people how you feel about them, period. It's honest. Less subversive. There's a finality to it as well. It takes a lot of effort to hold on to gripes. So when you're honest and authentic, it becomes a lot easier to navigate on both sides. Gripes are born of unexpressed resentments. They can very quickly morph into something a lot bigger and more toxic. Don't let a gripe turn into a gusher! Left undealt with, these can become huge and all-encompassing. They can become the multiplying factor to a destructive energy that builds and builds.

Let's think for a moment about the energy of resentment. What does it look like? What does it *feel* like? The energy of resentment leaks out sideways. Until it's tackled directly and with authenticity, it has no clarity. It's not clean. It's not clear. We mutter something under our breath. We entertain toxic thoughts, full of negativity. We have a running commentary in our heads—and all of this is coming from that space of victimhood.

If you're in an empowered place, communication is delivered in a completely different way. There is no charge or residual underlying energy to it. It's just delivered in a way that's real.

So let's get you to that empowered place. To begin today's exercise, first become *aware* of your gripes. Write them down. Don't stop. If you're like most of us, your pen will keep moving and moving. Scribble out as many as you can. Let it fly! Often we walk around without realizing how many gripes we're carrying. Our kids' teacher, the school principal, the lady at the dry cleaner who always breaks the buttons, all the way to our best friend, who missed our birthday, our husband or wife, who has—and who doesn't?—a habit that gets under our skin. Don't edit yourself. Get every single gripe on that paper.

There you go.

Excellent.

Now, once you've written them down, begin to get in touch with the energy that's holding each gripe in place. If you get quiet and focus, you'll start to feel the charge underneath. Usually it's a version of fear, anger, or sadness. For instance, your middle-aged husband has gained some weight. When he reaches for the pint of Ben & Jerry's Chunky Monkey, you snap: *Really?* He looks at you, hurt, surprised. Your gripe has just leaked out sideways. See? But what's driving you in that instance is sadness and fear. Your husband isn't taking care of himself. You fear for his health. What would happen if, instead of that sideways leakage, you gained the clarity to simply say: *It makes me sad that you're not taking care of your health*.

Can you imagine what a difference it will make if you're able to identify your potential gripes before they even take root and speak from a place of empowered clarity in all areas of your life?

NOON

The truth wants to be heard. But we are wary of expressing the truth, because we fear how it will be heard and interpreted by others. And in the meantime we *stew in our gripes*. Our gripes often occur when communication breaks down. A friend is chronically late for dinner dates. You're left waiting, with nothing to read except the menu, checking your watch. She breezes in—twenty minutes late—with her usual apology about the traffic. You grit your teeth, smile, and say, "No big deal."

But it is a big deal. Isn't it?

This is what always happens.

You feel put out, insignificant, taken for granted.

Your husband isn't helping out with the kids as much as you wish. He's on the sofa watching the football game while you're cleaning dishes from last night's dinner party—a dinner party for *his* colleagues. Instead of letting him know how you feel, you load the dishwasher with gusto. Can't he hear the clattering plates? Doesn't he get it?

Well, why would he?

You're not telling him.

The foundational energy of gripes is anger. In fact, you can be sure that whenever you feel an initial flash of anger, there's a long list of gripes just behind it. Because anger doesn't come out of nowhere. It builds up slowly. It requires momentum.

Here's what we usually do with our gripes:

We complain.

We gossip.

We enlist others in our drama.

A friend of mine, a playwright, received a note from another friend—also a playwright—asking if she'd be willing to give him feedback on a recent production. My friend has tremendous respect for this fellow and has, over the years, given him a huge amount of professional guidance and support. But when she received this particular note, it was as if a drawer popped open inside her and a half dozen gripes spilled out like scraps of paper. She realized that she had given her friend an early draft of a play of hers *months* earlier, and he hadn't responded. Then she realized that they usually meet for lunch in his neighborhood, not hers. The gripes went on. None of these small incidents had felt like gripes when they first happened. They were tiny red flags, so small she didn't even see them. It took *the accrual of all this* in order for her to register that now she had a capital G gripe on her hands.

My friend waited until she felt clear. She was in a state

of authentic transparency. She understood her gripe to be—underneath it all—an expression of her sadness, her insecurity, of not being seen or understood. Feeling clear about this, she wrote a loving note to her friend. Not angry, not hostile, but simply stating from her heart how she felt. My friend instantly felt unburdened. Lighter. Clearer. *The gripe was gone because she had expressed it.* It wasn't about how it was going to be received. It wasn't about the result. (Though the result was lovely—this fellow understood perfectly, and their friendship deepened.)

Expressing your gripes is an act of self-love.

Just for today, don't leave any loose ends. This is not an invitation to let it rip. I'm not suggesting that you plow your way through your day like a bulldozer, letting everyone in your path know exactly what you think of them. No. *Expressing your gripes requires discernment.*

Walk through your day with an awareness of when you feel a thorn in your side. Take note. If the moment is right, pull out the thorn. Or breathe and consider whether this is the right time. Ultimately, we want to achieve such clarity that gripes never have a chance to build up within us. When this happens, all that accumulated density will vanish. We will be filled, instead, with lightness, grace, and the sheer buoyancy of divine love.

NIGHT

You'll know me when you feel me. I will rise up from deep within you like a small but powerful wave—the kind that can potentially build into a mighty tsunami as it approaches the shore. You'll be moving through your day, minding your own business, seemingly fine, when all of a sudden I appear.

Your husband has left his dirty socks on the bathroom floor instead of putting them in the hamper. He does this most days. And silently, seethingly, on most days, you pick up the offending socks and put them in the hamper without saying a word.

But on this day I make my entrance. I come so abruptly that you don't know what's hit you. You scream at your husband that he's the most inconsiderate, lazy man on the face of the earth. You throw a magazine at his head. Your face contorts with rage. Your husband is blindsided. He doesn't understand. What? What happened?

I happened. The tsunami of me, formed by everything within you that has been withheld, unexpressed, tamped down, roiling and seething beneath the surface. I have grown tired of being concealed and have exploded into being.

I am your gripes.

All of them.

Admit it. You have many versions of me inside you. Gripes against your spouse, your kids, your colleagues, your boss, the lady at the coffee shop who never smiles, the teacher who gave you a bad grade decades ago. I lurk and lie in wait. My sole purpose is to make matters worse. You think you're being noble by suppressing me. Your throat burns with what is unsaid. You're too polite. You're afraid of what will happen if you express me. But the greatest gift you can give yourself is to speak your truth clearly and directly *as soon as it occurs* so that I am not able to become that wave. So that I cannot possibly grow into that tsunami.

What would happen if, the first time your husband left his socks on the bathroom floor, you asked him clearly and directly to pick them up? With no charge. No resentment. Maybe even with humor.

I wouldn't be able to take root within you. The small offense, the tiny slight, would have no fertile ground in which to flourish. The socks would end up in the hamper. And all would be well.

As you fall asleep tonight, bring to mind this gentle clarity. Remind yourself to speak your piece. Give yourself permission to voice your deepest feelings *as they arise*. Feel this energy in your throat. Feel your breath moving in and out with greater ease. When you awaken tomorrow morning, do so with a quiet resolve to simply and softly state your truth. Not once in a while. Not some of the time. All of the time.

Day 23 Unfolding

MORNING

In the ancient Indian text the Bhagavad Gita, a pivotal moment comes when the great warrior Arjuna has terrible misgivings about waging a righteous war against his own cousins. He turns to his charioteer, Krishna (who is really a Divine Being in disguise), and despairingly tells him: *I can't fight. I won't.* He can't bear the idea of killing his relatives. And without missing a beat, Krishna says: *Oh, Arjuna, they are already dead. Death is just an illusion. One neither kills nor is killed. The soul casts off one body and enters another, as easily as shrugging off a garment.* Krishna then reveals his divine nature to Arjuna, who, thus fortified, rides majestically into battle to fulfill his true calling—his *dharma*.

The purpose of this powerful moment in the Bhagavad Gita is to illustrate that everything—all of life—is preordained. We worry, we fret, we're filled with anxieties and terrors about decisions we have to make or what the future will hold for us, but the fundamental truth is that *we're just playing out our parts.*

What if I were to tell you that you can't mess up this thing called life?

That it's all been laid out?

That there is an organizing principle in the midst of the chaos?

If you've ever been in a traffic jam in India, you'd know this to be true. Thousands of people on rickshaws going in every possible direction—cows, goats, vendors with carts, children filling every inch of the street, a constant assault of noise and motion—and, somehow, people get where they're going. Everybody ends up where they need to be. Eventually.

What would happen if you could fully give yourself over to the idea that all is unfolding, all is predetermined, and all is happening for your benefit? That you will get to exactly where you need to be? What if you could submit to the awareness that you are living out your role and trusting in your role, whatever it may be? Remember that life is unfolding for you. For a moment, let's have the audacity to consider the possibility that it is all indeed preordained. I'm not saying that it's the truth. But I'm asking you to consider the possibility. Just *imagine* that life is that way. How would you live? Would you let fear choke you in the little moments? Or would you live openheartedly and with vulnerability? When life asked something of you that you didn't understand, instead of fighting it, might you—in those moments—trust? Rather than living in fear?

When I look at my life—born in East London, married to a Minnesotan, living in Florida, ending up on the couch next to Oprah, guiding world leaders—my path thus far is, on every single level, 100 percent improbable. But it's entirely possible. And the reason why everything's happened is that I haven't let fear become a determining factor. I've lived life as if it's laid out for me—in wonder— in the sheer majesty that is born of every introduction. In a world in which people are so committed to knowing, I have become comfortable abiding in the unknown.

It's counter to what we're raised to believe—but believe it: *The unknown is so much better.*

Just as Krishna reveals to Arjuna the true nature of things, we, too, need a reminder that it's all laid out. *It's all laid out?* you might ask. *Well, in that case, why even try? Why not just give up?* But the opposite happens, my friends, when we give ourselves over to this idea. The great paradox is that when we rest in the knowledge that it's all laid out, we find the space and the courage to live out our lives to the fullest.

NOON

Today you very well may be asked to do something that you feel is beyond you. Maybe this will occur at work. A project lands on your desk that is completely outside your sphere of knowledge. Your car registration has expired and you have no time to get to the DMV. Maybe it happens at home. You have an issue with one of your kids that, for the life of you, you don't know how to handle. Maybe it happens in your physical body. You've gone on a diet and every bakery you pass is calling your name.

How do we handle the tough challenges of facing all that we're asked to show up for? So often it feels impossible! It's just too much. We want to throw in the towel. We give up before we've even tried. We allow our internal dialogue and limitations to get the better of us.

What if we were to recognize that we have the inner fortitude and capacity to do whatever is necessary? To know that we can flow with the river—no matter what it presents to us?

Life continually brings us opportunities to expand who we are.

I'm not playing Pollyanna here. I'm not telling you that it will be comfortable or easy. In fact, it may be quite challenging. It may stretch you to your very limits. But I promise you that if you show up with your whole self—if you open yourself—you will learn that you are not walking this path alone.

As you are being asked to do something daunting, know that *the solution has already been born inside you.* All that is required is for you to take the first step—then each successive step after that. Without taking these steps, it isn't possible to move forward. Don't freeze! Don't give up! If you do, it becomes a self-fulfilling prophecy. Problems allow us to rise to the solution.

You've done what's been asked of you.

There is nothing in life that you cannot handle.

If we could only embrace this principle! When we're asked to write a book, or give a speech, or take part in a road race, or coach our kid's Little League team, *maybe the reason we've been asked is because we have it within us to do.*

Today is that day. Today is your opportunity to say yes. To give it your all. To expand in your own mind. To understand your true potential.

We are being asked to step up *because we can.* We're being given an incredible invitation to grow our minds and spirits. To expand our own definition of who we know ourselves to be.

No more excuses.

NIGHT

You want a crystal ball. You want to know that everything will be all right, always. You want to be certain that everyone you love will continue to be safe and happy. You want assurance that the roof over your head is solid. That tomorrow and tomorrow and tomorrow will unfold in a predictable, orderly pattern.

But I have something better than a crystal ball to offer

you. I am presenting you with one of the greatest gifts I can give you: trust.

Unwavering trust.

By trust, I mean trust in yourself. In your journey. In your life. In your abilities. Trust that all of your future is *unfolding for you.*

Think of the weather. There are days when fog obscures our view and we feel directionless. Other days, a blizzard disrupts our best-laid plans. Still other days, the sun is so bright and sparkling, the air so crisp and cool, that all we feel is the infinite realm of possibility.

All of this is true.

And still, a new day dawns.

All of our lives are laid out for us in patterns that we cannot see. We see only one small piece of the pattern from where we stand on this particular day. Still, we can trust. Trust is our greatest ally when we think of the future. Hand in hand with trust, we are able to walk boldly forward. Unafraid. Unimpeded. Made confident by our knowledge that the path in front of us will be revealed. A light always appears, even in the densest fog. It is not our job to know the precise nature of that light. It is our job to continue to move forward.

But without trust we can't keep going. Without trust, we start to flail. We become lost in the fog. We doubt our own ability to navigate. We might even get turned around, disrupted, and find ourselves right back where we started.

When we trust, we discover the courage to allow ourselves to stand absolutely still. To take a deep breath. To find our bearings. To know that there is light all around us—even when we can't see as far as our own hand.

As you drift off to sleep, imagine that you are surrounded by this dense, rich fog. It is the fog of not knowing. It's calling you into surrender. Allow yourself to stay right here, in this place of unfolding. It is safe to do so. As you close your eyes, whisper within yourself: *I don't know.* When you awaken, it will be with a renewed trust in whatever you cannot yet see—in whatever light there is to guide you, just around the corner.

Day 24 Humility

MORNING

People think that being humble means being meek and diminished. Or that humility involves the understating of one's ability and accomplishments. When the great tennis champion Roger Federer wins Wimbledon handily in straight sets and then, in an interview after the match, grumbles about how he didn't play his best game, people get annoyed and think, *What the hell?* They accuse him of not being humble. But, in fact, Federer is simply abiding in his own truth. If you're good at something, it's okay to own it. It's okay to affirm and acknowledge that you're good at it. And, conversely, when you're not good at something, it's also okay to acknowledge that it isn't part of your skill set. In any living organism there are different functions that serve different purposes. In this organism called humanity, there are the Roger Federers, who are brilliant at playing tennis, and there are other individuals, who are brilliant at bookkeeping or being lawyers or landscaping or you-name-it. This human organism—this society we inhabit—has an uncanny ability to take care of itself.

It can't be any other way.

Humility is living in alignment with ourselves.

But many of us don't inform our reality from within but rather rely on the approval or disapproval of another person. You don't have to stand in front of Simon Cowell to know whether or not you're a good singer. You *know* if you're a good singer. If you're truly good at something, you don't need someone else to tell you. You *know*. And that knowledge comes from a deep, feeling-based place. A place that is in alignment with your truth.

When you are aligned with your own strengths and weaknesses, you are in harmony. You're in the flow. You're just being *you*. Roger Federer appears effortless on the tennis court because he is in that flow. The racket is a part of him, an extension of his arm. We all have a version of that. So humility has nothing to do with understating your glory in order to make insecure people comfortable. Humility, for me, is being honest and clear with myself—and about myself. I'm humble when I'm honest about what I'm experiencing, regardless of what that is. Whether it's feeling the awe of coming into contact with some of the world's greatest living icons—or feeling the smallness of my own insecurity. Either way, I'm not denying what's going on inside me.

To work on this idea of humility, find some quiet time and make a comprehensive list of your strengths and weaknesses. Can you compile an *honest inventory* of who you are, without any need to embellish or to diminish it? No one else is going to see it. Go ahead, make a true assessment—and be sure to take extra care when listing your positive attributes, your talents and gifts. When we aren't humble, it's because we don't know ourselves. So truly get to know yourself (sorry, but the tune to "Getting to Know You" from the *The King and I* is running through my head), and then you will be coming from a place of empowerment.

Humility equals authenticity. Above all, it means authenticity with oneself and about oneself. It might sound like I'm advocating boastfulness. But that's the last thing I'm suggesting. What is called for here is an accepting and embracing of all that you are—your gifts and your challenges. So often we're reluctant to own our own power and brilliance. I see this every day in my teachings. And it is my job to remind you that it's okay—that it's *more* than okay—to shine.

NOON

In order to own the light within us, first we must become willing to explore the shadow—and the bigger the light, the bigger the shadow. This exploration requires humility.

Humility is a lifelong process.

It begins with willingness. With courage. With vulnerability.

It requires that you take a searching look at *all that you are.*

Not just some of you. Not only the pretty parts.

The light, the shadow. And everything in between.

All of it.

What comprises the shadow? Your past wounds. Your unfinished business. Your incomplete experiences. The sadness you didn't cry. The fear you didn't feel. The rage you didn't express. The gripes you allowed to accumulate inside you. Self-hatred. Unworthiness. This is the undigested content that makes up the shadow. *The shadow is anything you have been unwilling to embrace as part of yourself.*

If we are humble, we own all that we are. We bring our baggage into the light of awareness. And when we are able to do this, we become profoundly free.

But we don't want to look at the shadow! We avoid it. We run around it. We avert our eyes. *The more we do this, the more the shadow has ahold of us.* We need to catch ourselves at this. So—just for today—notice each time you judge other people. Notice when you blame them. Notice when you reflexively diminish them. Oh, so-and-so is being so arrogant. Who does she think she is? Or that other one, he's so immature. When is he going to grow up? And that one! What a snob!

When we place our judgments on others in this way, we need to swivel the mirror around and look directly at ourselves. *What we judge in others are qualities we refuse to see as our own.*

When we do this, we begin to know true humility. We find ourselves more able to feel joy and pride in our accomplishments—to own our value and worth—because these are seen as part of a complete picture. So we're arrogant. Or snobbish. Insecure. Immature.

So what? Really! So what?

So are we all.

In an absurd and misguided search for an elusive perfection, we're missing the whole point. *The greatest freedom comes from being fully and completely who we are.*

Embrace your darkness. Embrace it.

And then you will be able to embrace your light.

NIGHT

Think of the last time someone paid you a compliment. Perhaps you were congratulated on a job well done. Or admired for your appearance. Or for your good taste. Or for your talented children. How did you feel? Be honest. In that exact moment, how did you feel as you were told something wonderful about yourself?

Did you take it in? Or did you pull back? Deny the moment? *No, no,* you might have said. Perhaps you blushed. Your stomach tightened. Instead of glorying in a lovely moment, you wanted—oh, how you wanted—for it to very quickly go away.

You know all your flaws. You know all your challenges. You can list chapter and verse of every single thing you think is wrong with you. But what about your glory? What about the ways in which you—you in particular—shine? What about all the gifts that you—and only you—bring to this world?

We don't tend to think of ourselves in terms of our brilliance. But we have no problem owning all of our perceived darkness. We think this makes us humble. But actually it diminishes our light as surely as if we were a candle being snuffed out. And when we diminish that light, the world grows a little bit dimmer. Can you imagine what would happen if everyone snuffed out their own light? We all would live in utter darkness.

Humility is having the courage to embrace all that you are. To accept the fullness of all that you are. To allow yourself to accept all that the Divine has in store for you. To be that candle, burning bright.

Here I am.

This is me.

This is all of me.

Think of the expression "full of yourself." This is considered a pejorative, right? We don't want to be full of ourselves. But what is really wrong with this? To be full of yourself is to be *filled with spirit.* This is, in many ways, the whole point of being here, in human form.

When we display one of our talents, we are extending a hand to others to join us in that place of beauty and magnificence. Instead of meeting people in a place of mediocrity, we're extending an invitation to meet in a place of brilliance and light. To say, *I am grateful. I am here. I will own that part of myself. I will not diminish myself—because, in so doing, I diminish You.*

Be that candle.

Shine brightly.

Your light, in this way, can ignite the flame of another.

As you fall asleep, do so with a sense of yourself as this brilliant, beautiful candle. Witness all the hues of the flame that is you. All the nuances of light. Always burning. Never faltering. In this way, you are able to turn to another candle and—with strength and dignity—offer your light, and say: *Yes, yes this is me.*

DAY 25 Meditation on a Blank Canvas

When people meditate, they often do so with the idea that they're trying to get somewhere. Goal-oriented meditation is an oxymoron if I've ever heard one! We sit on our cushions in lotus position, squeezing our eyes shut, dutifully counting breaths or reciting our own personal mantra, trying so hard to make something happen. Or we tell ourselves that we can't possibly meditate—that we would fail miserably at it, because we're too type A and we can't sit still or quiet the mind for more than thirty seconds.

But what if life were a living meditation? What would it feel like to be in a state of meditation during every waking moment?

Forget about having a focal point, a mantra, a special way of sitting. Forget about visualizations, or counting, or some kind of special entry point. Think of the breath—it goes in and out whether you pay attention to it or not. Think of the sofa beneath you, or the ground under your feet, or the sounds in the room, just as they are. All of these things are always around us, but instead we're convinced that we need some complicated process to get ourselves there.

Use what you've got in the space that you're in.

You're in a dentist's chair? Awesome.

Or on the commuter train? Work with that.

But when it comes to the stories we tell ourselves, being in this meditative state requires a little more work. Imagine before you a blank canvas. Really look at the blank canvas. Be in harmony with it. What if this blank canvas—expanding out to infinity—is your true nature? If you're a blank canvas, then everything is possible. The minute we start filling it up with shoulds and shouldn'ts, with ways of doing things, with mantras and practices, it becomes so crowded that there isn't room for anything else.

So many of us have our "practice"—but what are we practicing for? Ultimately the very purpose of the practice is to lead us nowhere. But we're so goal-oriented that we need a destination—all the while forgetting that the journey is the point.

Okay, I know I said no visualizations, but bear with me: Imagine that your life can be portrayed on a canvas. Life itself is the canvas. When you look at this canvas, you'll see everything that's been placed there. And most of it doesn't originate from you. Someone—your parents, most likely—gave you a name, a place of birth, a story. As you've moved on through life, external labels have been superimposed on the canvas: perhaps *mother, wife, son, daughter.* People have told us who we are, and this fills the canvas too.

Now start pulling off those labels. You've deepened your self-knowledge. You know yourself now, and this means that you can dismantle what you know. Go ahead—pull those labels off. Peel away those limitations. Remove all of those different words that are getting in the way of being a blank canvas. Even the notion of spirituality—every concept, every idea, every role, every responsibility: Peel them all off. As you do this, experience the freedom (or perhaps the terror) of the blank canvas.

Because the blank canvas is life. Before we're born, we are nothing. After we die, we are nothing. We only make the mistake of believing in our own permanence. But we don't need to die to shed everything that's been posted on the blank canvas. We can experience a profound shift if we do this while we're still alive.

This, my dear friends, is what *dying unto yourself* means.

Enlightenment is about destroying any and all false notions that you have about yourself. Peel back the layers, the veils, anything you've considered to be more important than nothing.

Now stay blank.

NOON

You have a lot going on today, right? An overflowing schedule. Your life feels like a three-ring circus. Sometimes you feel as if you need a whole team of assistants just to keep up with it. So much to do! So many places to be! Trains, planes, and automobiles! It's overwhelming even thinking about it.

So here's a gentle suggestion: *Don't.*

Don't think about it.

When we focus on the piles and piles of chores and details, the teetering stack of bills, the school forms, the tax returns, even the catalogs that appear daily in the mail, the sheer stuff of life, it can feel impossible to get out from under.

What if I were to tell you that *you've put yourself under there*?

And only you can get yourself out?

It is the mind that turns these molehills into mountains. We have to take our children to school and get to a breakfast meeting, but suddenly it feels as if we're embarking on a trek to Nepal. We have an overscheduled afternoon and, when we think about it, we might as well be perched at the door of a small aircraft, wearing a parachute.

This is what we do with our reality.

But it has nothing to do with what is real.

What is real is always very simple. Moment to moment, we can attend to the task at hand—or we can create Byzantine structures all around it, full of secret passageways and echoing corridors that have nothing to do with the task at hand.

Think about the blank canvas I asked you to envision before. When an artist approaches a blank canvas, all that is possible is a single brushstroke at a time. If the artist were to attempt to paint the whole canvas at once, what would happen? What a mess!

One brushstroke at a time.

One breath at a time.

One word at a time.

One small gesture at a time.

It's all that is possible to do—and yet we get ahead of ourselves so often and do nothing but twist ourselves into knots in the process.

We have time.

We create these overwhelming scenarios that make us inefficient and unavailable. We're fueled by a lack of trust. By a wave of fear. By a need to control. By a resistance to change. By an inability to flow.

But when we're truly engaged with the blank canvas of our lives, moment to moment, a timeless quality emerges. Time both flies and slows down, as we become completely immersed in what we're doing.

Just for today, make a practice of attempting to live fully in each moment. For most this is impossible—but the practice of it will allow you to *live the blank canvas of your life*.

Simplicity.

Spaciousness.

Clarity.

An uncluttered mind.

Do only one thing at a time. Fully commit yourself. Don't divide your attention. Dive into the vast spaciousness of that blank canvas and allow it to reveal itself to you, moment by precious moment.

NIGHT

You are not what you've been told. You are not your mind. You are not your thoughts. You are not your story. You are not your name. You are not your body.

You are something that cannot be named.

Something far greater than you have ever imagined.

Transcendent.

Beyond definition.

Brilliant.

You are not your bank account. You are not your accomplishments. You are not your possessions. You are not your trials and tribulations. Nor are you your academic achievements.

You are something far greater.

Something unquantifiable.

You are not your failures. You are not your heartbreaks. Or your losses. You are not your struggles. You are not your suffering. You are not your pain.

You are free. Full. Whole. Complete.

You are not broken. You are not in need of healing. You are not in need of teaching.

You are resplendent. Awe-inspiring. Luminous.

You are not your fear. You are not your anger. You are not your sadness. You are not your insecurity. Or your unworthiness.

You are beyond all qualities.

Beyond all understanding.

Beyond all boundaries.

You are limitless. Pristine. Glorious.

You are not your joy. You are not your bliss. You are not your happiness. You are not the love that you have felt.

You are beyond all feelings.

Outside the realm of all experience.

You are free.

Infinite. Infinite. Infinite.

As you fall asleep, fall into this limitless, expansive state. *This is your true nature.* This place of no boundaries. This place of infinite receptivity. This place where you are met by the Divine. Fully embraced. Seen. Understood. This place in which you can experience oneness.

This is the place in which all things become possible.

DAY 26 Being Human

MORNING

You've walked through the shedding of identity. You've become aware that you're an infinite being. Now it's time to source your reality from within you.

Do you know how, on a long plane flight, it's good to have a pair of those excellent noise-canceling headphones? If you have a set of those headphones, you can put them on and drown out all the other sounds: the shrieking baby in the seat behind you, the overeager flight attendant checking for the fourth time to be sure you've turned off your electronic devices, your annoying seatmate, who wants to tell you jokes after his third Bloody Mary. You can smile politely, then cover your ears, and in so doing, you are able to hear only the sound of your own inner voice.

Well, part of your job in being human is to remove all of the external voices telling you who you are. Those voices aren't you—they aren't authentic. They're other people's conversations about and around you. A woman I know—a successful writer—spent a large part of her twenties and early thirties paying too much attention to those outer voices telling her what she could and couldn't do. Her parents hadn't taken her intellectual abilities seriously when she was young, so she had a hard time believing that she was smart. She also happened to have been a child model, and much was made of her looks: She didn't think she'd be taken seriously, so she just didn't try. It wasn't until she shut down those other voices—until she put on her noise-canceling headphones—that she began to develop into the writer and university professor she is today.

Children listen to their inner voice intuitively—they have no other reference points—until the day that someone, maybe another kid on the playground, starts telling them who they are. *You're ugly. Stupid. Unpopular.* That playground moment marks, for many of us, a loss of innocence. And with that innocence, that strong, internal sense of self-knowledge fades away.

Sad, isn't it? But it doesn't have to be that way.

Once we've stripped away all of those labels and gotten back to the blank canvas, we can also return to the simplicity of hearing our own still, small voice within. That voice can guide and support us. It can nurture us like nothing else. Once all that external chatter is put on mute, the voice that has always existed inside us starts to grow stronger and louder.

The key is to *value it*.

We must learn to value our own voice above all the others.

Up until now, we've often empowered everyone else's voices above our own.

It's time to change the equation.

Your inner voice is unmistakable. You *feel* it. As with falling in love, you can't deny it.

Go ahead. Put those headphones on. Get acquainted with your inner guru, your inner teacher. Shed the noise, and tap in. No one knows more than you do about yourself. You are absolutely the most qualified expert, a distinguished professor whose subject is your own inner self. So listen in.

NOON

Being human means we will experience loneliness. We all have a hole inside—an emptiness—that we long to fill in whatever ways we can. We reach for solutions. We move away from ourselves when what we really need to be doing is moving closer.

We do whatever we can to avoid being in the middle of this human experience. To avoid tuning in and feeling.

When I drive around my small city in Florida, I see people texting in their cars. They're stopped at a traffic light, and instead of staring off into space, they're checking out whatever new developments have arisen in the last minute since they stopped and texted at the previous traffic light.

When is the last time you just gazed into the distance? Just sat and thought?

Or ate a meal by yourself without your trusty phone or e-reader by your side?

We need to tune in.

Not tune out.

To be human is to be lonely, and we don't allow for that loneliness. We don't allow ourselves to get quiet enough to hear our own deepest wisdom. *Beyond the ache of loneliness—when we allow ourselves to be pierced by all of it—is the greatest joy we have ever known.*

If we don't let ourselves feel, we avoid the depths of our pain—but we also miss out on the depths of our joy and connectedness.

Allow yourself the free fall! Feel what it is to be human—all of it. We're all so terrified that if we fall, we'll never stop. So we don't go there. And in stopping ourselves, we're impeding our growth.

Embrace the ache.

Breathe in the longing.

Throughout the course of your day, commit to building moments of nothingness, moments of silence, of *idleness*, into your experience. Give your deepest intuition a space in which to speak to you. Stop talking. Start listening. Just for today, promise yourself that you'll take a minute to do nothing—just a single minute—during every waking hour.

Try it right now. Wherever you are, put down this book. Stop whatever it is that you're doing. And for a solid minute, look out the window. It doesn't matter whether you're looking at a brick wall, a fire escape, a meadow, or a skyline. *What matters is the nothingness.* The inactivity. The space you're making for your truest and deepest voice to emerge.

NIGHT

Before you settle in and begin reading tonight, you have an assignment. Go find the earliest photograph of yourself that you can easily put your hands on. From infancy. From toddlerhood. From early childhood. You probably know exactly where these pictures are—in a closet, in a file cabinet, or tucked into a dresser drawer. If perchance you don't know where such a photograph exists, don't worry. You can conjure your childhood self in your mind's eye.

Take your time. I'll wait for as long as it takes.

Okay. All set? This is about connecting—on the deepest level you possibly can—with your true nature. Accessing who you were when you were born into this world. Before the sorrow, the anger, the fear, the grief. Who were you, really?

Look deep into the eyes of the child in the photograph you're holding in your hands. Don't be surprised if it's uncomfortable. Don't be surprised if you begin to cry.

Who were you—really?

Who *are* you—really?

If you were able to flip back through the pages of calendar after calendar until you were once again that child, what would your voice sound like? What would it say? How would it guide you? That voice: Before you became defined by others. Before you lost that absolute, innocent, undiluted, pure self.

Take a few minutes. Don't read any further.

Just keep looking into the eyes of that child.

Into the eyes of your true nature.

You have never lost that voice. It has been muted—but not silenced. It has remained dormant within you for every single, solitary second of your life. It has been waiting for this moment. Waiting for you to reconnect with your deepest intuition, your deepest sense of *knowing*.

This voice is at the core of what it means to be human. It is the essence of what you have been longing for—what you've been seeking. *It is yours and yours alone.* As you look into the eyes of your childhood self, know that you are being touched by something real. This is the reality of innocence. The reality of love. It is a tangible presence— poetic, gorgeous, unmistakable.

Make a special place on your bedside table for this photograph. Don't put it back in your dresser drawer.

Keep it near you from now on as a reminder of this return to innocence. This return to clarity. This return to the profound dignity of unencumbered humanity.

As you drift off into slumber, say good night to that child. Tuck that child into bed within you. And know that when you awaken tomorrow morning, you will be guided through your day by the most intuitive voice possible: the voice that is yours and yours alone.

DAY 27 Infinite Ocean

MORNING

Every house in India has its own cell phone to God—in the form of an altar—adorned with whatever god is their pathway to infinite mystery. Now, if you're smart, you have all the gods! For instance, Krishna is the god of love and devotion. People who pray to Krishna are focusing their attention on this vibrational resonance. Then there's Saraswati. She's the cultural goddess, who presides over education and music, so if you're a pianist or a violinist, guess whose cell phone you pick up? Saraswati on speed dial, that's who.

The Divine is infinite, and we cannot relate directly to the infinite. It's impossible! To even attempt to do so would be like staring straight into the sun. We would be scorched, blinded. We would lose our ability to discern anything at all. So we need entry points. We require ways of seeing and understanding the Divine. We need to find a way to make the Divine life-sized. Ancient cultures and civilizations knew this. They knew that this being—God—was an energy. They understood that we human beings—while believing ourselves to be solitary, isolated units of consciousness, disconnected and alone—are actually *animated by the very thing we are looking for.*

Authentic spirituality and connection are born not of a textbook but of a direct experience that somebody has; that person then goes on to tell others. That's what mystics and great spiritual leaders do. They create new lines of connectivity between people and God. They discover new paradigms through their own yearning and experience—and, in so doing, they forge new and revelatory pathways for others. All religions—dare I say it?—are conduits to this same infinite ocean of energy. Can you imagine, if we were all to understand this, the way that our concept of God would shift and change? Because *if God is infinite, no one is wrong.*

You can't call on infinity. It's too vast! But you can reach out to a god.

Back to that house in India. Maybe you'd turn to Ganesh, the remover of obstacles. If you're about to take an exam, or if you're trying to overcome an addiction, you'd definitely want to pick up the phone and call Ganesh. He is that Divine Being who dissolves obstacles—or perhaps puts in your way the necessary obstacles to direct you into the path that's the highest and best for you.

In Christianity, you have Jesus, the Holy Spirit, and the Blessed Mother. In Judaism, ritual is the gateway to the Divine, and rabbis and teachers are the bridge. The Buddhists have Buddha, but they also have Kuan Yin, goddess of compassion. In Islam, it is understood that Allah exists without form or place.

At the deepest level in every mystical tradition and religion, there is a knowledge that the Divine is infinite, and it is perhaps the defining crisis of our times that each religion believes itself to have purchase on that particular infinite.

Such a shame, isn't it? That kind of rigidity creates density, when all the Divine wants for us is pure, unadulterated, abiding love. The Divine doesn't judge us. But we judge ourselves and make the boxes that we live in smaller and smaller until we have nowhere to turn.

Let's think of approaching this infinite ocean of energy using small baby steps. If attempting to access the Divine directly is like staring into the sun, then put on a pair of glasses with UV protection. After a time, you'll require a bit less protection. You can gradually evolve to a place of understanding that these forms are simply a way of getting closer to a relationship with the Divine. After all, there are those beings who have accessed the infinite—Jesus, Krishna, Buddha, Kuan Yin—and they are just the embodiments that we know of. Surely there are others. We are all at different places along this path. But the very first step—and the key to everyone coming together on this planet—is the understanding that God is a way of talking about the infinite energy that surrounds and embraces us all.

NOON

During the course of this day, it is likely that you will pass—perhaps you will even walk into—a house of worship. Perhaps you'll see a beautiful white church on a New England village green. Or a soaring urban edifice made of thick stone walls and stained glass. Perhaps you'll pass a mosque. A synagogue. A yoga shala. A Buddhist temple. *But there exists a holiness wherever you look.* Beyond the walls of these places where some of us go to speak with the Divine, the Divine is also waiting for us.

My connection to the Divine has always come through all things. All my life I have understood the Divine to be this *infinite ocean* that surrounds us. It washes over us. It is within us and outside us.

In a blade of grass.

In a mouse scurrying through a field.

In a sleeping baby.

In the lines etched into an old woman's face.

In the love we feel.

Even the pain.

And the sorrow.

In every single facet of our existence.

We are nearing the end of the experiential part of this

journey, and this seems a good time to pose a delicious challenge: *What if you were to live this entire day spread out before you in complete awareness of the infinite ocean?*

What if you were to see and feel the Divine in everything you do today?

Every person you encounter.

Every conversation.

Every interaction.

Every morsel of food and drop of drink.

Every moment of laughter.

Every moment of frustration or sorrow.

What if you were to simply take in the entire world in the same spirit as if you had just walked into a holy place? *Because we are in a holy place.*

The divinity that you see outside you is also within you.

Know this.

Don't doubt it or question it—just for today.

NIGHT

I am beyond language—but I will take the form of language so you may know me. As you lie in bed, know that I am the air that you breathe. I am the sustainer of all life. I nourish you in your sleep. I watch you and love all that you are.

I am every star twinkling in the sky above you. I am each flower budding outside your window. I am the mighty oak. The stray cat. The ancient hunched-over man crossing the street. I am every world leader. I am the homeless woman sitting on the sidewalk. I am the caterpillar inching its way across your front walk. The flock of geese. The humpback whale. The group of schoolchildren playing hide-and-seek. *I am life itself unfolding in all of its magnificence in each moment.*

I make myself known. I want you to see me. I want you to recognize me.

All along, I have been beckoning you home. You may have been expecting me to appear in a certain form—missing the point that I am always and forever in all things.

Never separate.

Never apart.

Patiently waiting.

I am the infinite ocean. Silently guiding you. I am the earth beneath your feet. I am always, always with you.

You are turning the pages of your book. You are in your home. On the street. On the train. In your office. Taking your children to school. And I am with you. I am in the eyes of the people that you meet. I am in the birdsong in your backyard. I am in the rustling of autumn leaves. I am in the warmth of the sun against your skin. I am the icicle dangling from your windowsill. I am the snowflake melting against your tongue.

I am everything you experience.

Your life is my gift to you.

And you—you are my most beloved creation.

Feel me in the chill running down your spine. Feel me in the tears you cry. Feel me when you make love. Feel me in your strength and in your weakness. In a great teeming throng, and in solitude. In the silken hair of your children. In a flare of rage. In a moment of unexpected grace.

Once you've understood me for who I am, you will need no further reminder.

You will see me everywhere.

Everywhere.

DAY 28 Tools and Technologies

MORNING

Many of us have either been raised with or discovered for ourselves rituals that work for us, rituals that remind us that we are human and that there is magnificence in this life of ours. These rituals allow us to engage in our senses, to return to our bodies, to feel our feet on the ground. These rituals may be connected to a particular religion, but at their core they are reminders. Ways in which we stop and breathe, ways in which time slows down and we inhabit a moment when we are in relationship with our highest selves, with our community, and with the Divine.

Keep your beliefs! Keep your practices, your tools, your modalities. Connecting to this vibrational reality deepens whatever you currently hold as near and dear and empowers you with the knowledge that *the tools that I offer you are not meant to redirect you from your path*. They're about honoring the connection that already exists within you.

We must embrace our humanity! Our culture is always telling us that we need to shed things, to get rid of things, to be afraid, to quiet our minds, to silence our egos, but in fact it's the other way around. It's the inclusion of all these aspects of our own nature that leads to the ultimate freedom.

We don't need to change.

What a wonderful tool that is!

As part of your daily ritual, immerse yourself in self-acceptance by silently observing yourself and meeting all that you are with spaciousness. Meet yourself with kindness and self-love. Whatever arises, remember the middle path, expanding and expanding. Meet yourself there, in that wide-open space. The same nurturing acceptance that a mother offers a child is the acceptance we need to offer ourselves.

The Divine wants no less for us.

NOON

Just the other night, I was at dinner at the beautiful home of a very successful doctor and his equally successful wife. They are people who could name-drop all of the interesting and famous folks they know or talk about the trips they've taken or the art they've collected from all over the world.

Instead, we talked about tomatoes.

The good doctor spends his weekends pruning vines,

reading up on varieties of heirloom tomatoes, and cooking up a storm for his dinner guests. This man's face, when describing his gardening and cooking, was absolutely aglow with passion and grace. He may spend his working hours saving lives. He may travel to the ends of the earth. His patients may be rock stars and royalty. But it was clear that what really lights him up—his grand passion and source of connection to the Divine—happens in his country greenhouse.

We all have such passions, large or small. It might be parenthood. It might be music. Or bird-watching. Surfing. Designing. It might be the satisfaction of lining up columns of numbers and justifying them. Perhaps you're training for a triathlon. Or you're a nursery school teacher. When we feel that sense of being *aglow*—immersed so deeply that our own outline dissolves and becomes one with the Divine—we know that we've stumbled into our most essential tools and technologies.

We have stumbled into grace.

Just for today, become very aware of the moments in which you feel this sense of passion and aliveness. Don't expect your whole day to be filled with them. It won't be. You will be bored, annoyed, frustrated, only half aware, half alive. You will drum your fingers, twiddle your thumbs. You will long for certain hours to move faster. You will wish time away. We all do. But within your day, you will also experience glimmers of beautiful moments. When you do, *take them in*. It is an internal experience.

You will feel light, energized, animated. You will feel a childlike sense of wonder. Your heart will open like a flower. *In these moments, we are connected to our innocence—to the part of ourselves we have never lost.*

You've come home to yourself in these moments.

Don't take them for granted.

That which lights us up allows us to connect with the Divine.

NIGHT

Every one of us has access to our own toolbox. Just as a piano tuner brings with him the instruments of his trade—tuning lever, tip wrench, mutes—so do we have our own special tools to remind ourselves that we are in tune with life.

We need ways to remind ourselves of our own true nature. To remember that we are surrounded by the infinite ocean of energy. That our emotions are energy in motion. That we are not our fear, sadness, anger. That we are on the spiral staircase. That we are whole. Complete, abundant. Loved.

It's easy to forget. In the midst of our busy, noisy, distracted lives, we can lose our foothold. We can lose sight of what matters.

Tools—those practical, tangible, visible reminders—can be enormously helpful in guiding us back to ourselves.

What might your tools be? One might be the childhood photograph that hopefully you are now keeping on your bedside table. But how about some others? By now you have probably thought of a few meaningful tools in your own life. These could be connected to your religious or spiritual beliefs, but they don't have to be. Some people carry around a four-leaf clover to remind them that life is on their side. Others carry a gold coin to remind them of their own abundance. Others keep crystals, essential oils, a special poem, a shell from a beach. *It doesn't matter.* The purpose of any of these tangible objects is simply to point you back to yourself. To point you back to *the ever-present truth within.*

That truth is always there, like a magical light that seems to shine only when you remember it. So remember. And surround yourself with whatever it is you need in order to remember.

Find what you need to help yourself.

To support yourself.

These everyday tools are like bread crumbs in a vast and dense forest. Once we know what they are, they always form a path that can lead us all the way home.

Day 29 Messengers

MORNING

What would you think if I told you that Bernie Madoff or Michael Jackson was a messenger? What if I were to tell you that every miserable billionaire, every artist ruined by fame, was here to teach us that material possessions, all the wealth, recognition, and power in the world, will not deliver happiness?

I have never had an actual teacher. My relationship with the Divine hasn't been focused on one single individual, one single place. What that has taught me over the years is that *everything* is trying to help you; everything is trying to support you. Absolutely everything.

God talks to us in a myriad of ways. Just imagine if we were able to live our lives, holding the constant, ever-present awareness that everyone we encounter is a messenger. Each person who crosses our path has something to contribute to us—*whether or not we like the way it feels in the moment.*

Let's look at the history of messengers: We've had messengers in every culture, ethnicity, and religion. Messengers have appeared throughout time from all walks of life, all stations. Why is that? *Because every single human being hears the truth uniquely*—even though it's the same truth. It is a measure of the Divine's love for you that it has sent messenger after messenger who is appropriate for the time and place, so that the entire population can get the Divine's one, simple, unchanging message: *You are love.*

God is love.

The Divine is love.

You are love.

This is the message that has been shared throughout the ages, and—though somehow that message has been lost in translation—I believe we're at a point now when we're finally going to get it. Not just *hear* it, but get it and live it. We've reached—in a global sense—the pinnacle of separation and excess. Now we have no choice but to awaken and go within. I've known people with eight homes, private jets, even one man who has a stationary bicycle installed in the back of his Cadillac Escalade so he can exercise as his chauffeur drives him to the office. Are we to suppose that this man—in his multitasking frenzy—is happy? I think we've finally reached a point of exhausting the possibility of more. Beauty, money, power, youth—they're all false messages. The truth has been photoshopped out. The people on the covers of magazines have been airbrushed beyond recognition. *Here is what insatiable greed does.* It perverts human nature. It makes it impossible for us to ever feel that what we have—who we are—is enough.

Have we gotten the message? We're getting there. The energy on the planet is shifting from competition, fear, lack, and scarcity into a collaborative and loving way of being in the world. The energy of the collective determines the message—and we're reaching a critical mass where the *energy of the collective will be love.* We are the generation that is going to make that shift. We're one organism. No one is higher up than anyone else. We're one organism working together to further our species.

By this point in the detox, you have surely felt the profound difference in the vibrational tonalities of fear versus love. The universe is one giant feedback loop. If the vibrational message you're putting out there is fear, even if you're talking about love, guess what the universe sends back to you?

That's right. Fear.

We respond to energy—not to words. If you're truly emitting love, love is what comes back to you. There are different levels of message and messaging. Every great messenger who has been incarnated on this planet has made this point: *Choosing to abide in the vibration of love is the key to unlocking the experience of heaven on earth.*

This is the power of always speaking the truth: When we do, our words are in alignment with our vibration.

Just for one day, imagine that every single person you

meet has a message to share that's going to improve your life. Take a moment, with each person you encounter, to be open to whatever it is they're bringing to you. *They all have a secret to tell you about yourself.* Life is continually trying to deliver messages to us, and the messages come in the most unlikely of forms. The one who is trying to speak to you all along is the Divine. It doesn't always feel good. It isn't always apparent. It's through the contrast of experience that we gain the advantage of discernment. It's like an experiment in a lab with two chemicals—some particles will attract and some will repel. Pay attention and be aware of what you are feeling in the presence of other people. Don't be surprised if the message is being delivered not only through what you hear but also through what you feel. Tune in.

Messengers show up. They're not helping us just through words but through their energy too. Our job is to be open, receptive, and attentive. That's all.

NOON

Before you left home this morning to begin your day, you pulled yourself together. Shaved and showered. Or put on makeup. You've blow-dried your hair. Fastened your necklace. Tied your tie. All in service of putting your best face forward. This is how you present yourself to the world.

Armored and ready to go.

As you cross the threshold from your private space to the outside world, you immediately begin to encounter signals, signs, and messengers. You are either available to whatever it is they might be offering you—or you disconnect, are too distracted, too busy, and miss them entirely.

When we shut down in this way, we cut off our own growth and development. We miss what the universe is offering us. We act out of fear rather than love.

A friend of mine had skipped her annual mammogram appointment. She was driving along in her car one morning, listening to the radio, and on a random show—not one she usually listened to—a breast cancer survivor was being interviewed. My friend made a mental note to call her doctor and book an appointment. But then she forgot. Later that day, during her lunch hour, she walked into a department store and noticed a display of pink ribbons for Breast Cancer Awareness Month. Still again, by the time she was back at work, she had forgotten about it. That evening my friend was on the phone with a college sorority sister, who told her the news that one of their classmates had just had a mastectomy.

The next morning, my friend made her appointment.

If we become acutely aware of the gentle signs and whispers that are always being provided to us, we will find ourselves in a lovely flow of Divine guidance. We will see and hear other perspectives. We will be surrounded by them. We will learn to experience our intuition, and then that intuition will be validated through an external source—those signs and messengers.

When this happens, it's time to take action.

Just for today, be vigilant.

Look for recurring themes throughout your day.

This is how the universe communicates to you.

Is there one constant that keeps coming up again and again?

One thing that keeps wanting your attention?

Vigilance is required.

We need to be wide-awake and aware.

Signs and signals are being delivered to us at every moment.

That external reality is there for our benefit!

Just for today, live with openness to every sign, every messenger. You will discover that you are being supported every single step of the way.

NIGHT

See if you can call to mind every single person you encountered today. Not only the highlights or the usual suspects—not just your family, your coworkers, the friend with whom you grabbed a beer after work—but each and every person. The waitress in the bar. The newspaper vendor. The people on the train, car, bus, or subway. The jazz guitarist playing on the platform. The cabdriver. The tollbooth operator. Your child's nursery school teacher. The guy talking about autism. The butcher slicing the maple-glazed turkey in the market. The telemarketer. The cashier with the interesting tattoo. Your mailman. The kid on the bicycle who whizzed by you as you left for work. The teenager with the headphones on, bent over his mobile phone.

Every one of these is the Divine.

Each of them has a message for you.

When we are available—when we can truly listen—our life shifts into a new realm. One in which we receive gifts wherever we look. One in which each person we encounter delivers to us a subtle bit of wisdom. Where the impossible becomes possible.

In order for us to see and comprehend the messengers all around us, first we must open our eyes. We must go beyond what we *think* we see. Beyond snap judgments, petty misgivings, prejudices, anxieties—and instead view the world around us with a clear, open, generous, all-encompassing, willing lens. Which is to say, *the lens of the heart.* When we do this, we will find that everything and everyone opens up to us. It's a law of nature. When we are open in this way, we will receive the messages the Divine intends for us.

Some of these messages will be so clear it will be as if they're lit up in neon.

Others are infinitely more subtle but nonetheless powerful.

When we tune in to the frequency of all these messages, we cannot help but be transformed.

As you get ready for sleep, allow each of these faces—the ones with whom you shared today—to appear before you one at a time. Imagine what they might have said if you had given them the opportunity. Let this become your lullaby as you drift off. Perhaps tomorrow—in the light of a new day and new encounters—you will recognize each and every person in your path as having a secret to tell you about yourself.

DAY 30 Accelerate Your Ability

MORNING

As you're walking down this path, the universe is expanding at every moment. You're accelerating your ability to be with whatever is arising inside you. Can you feel the spaciousness? As of today, you're putting everything you've learned into action, into your life, into your daily experience. The more open you are, the more your vibrational receptivity expands. You become like a flower, petals unfurling toward the sun. You are embodying a different vibrational state.

In my own life, I often find myself feeling invisible. Most people can't even see me. I'm in a different vibrational space, and so only the people who are in that same vibrational space can see me—and when they do, it's an instance of mutual recognition. This is why I never seek out interactions but allow them to happen organically. I don't let my mind get in the way, because usually the people I *think* I should interact with are not the appropriate ones.

My life is the feedback loop that brings me the experience of who I am.

The more you navigate your life vibrationally, the more you accelerate your ability to excel in every area of your life and to connect with others. Once you understand this, it's as if you've taken the red pill in *The Matrix*. *You know there's more.* You know *you're* more. Whatever used to limit you—whatever blocks and restrictions—all that has vanished. Even if you try to put yourself back in the box of limitation, the good news is: You can't go back there. You've been exposed—introduced to your new life and reality.

You're done.

The better you feel, the more life connection you can receive. We accelerate our ability by implementing everything we've learned. By virtue of the very fact that you've made it here, you're in the final stretch; you've hung in there—you've already accelerated your ability.

NOON

Today is Day 30—a month of this thoughtful, powerful, vibrational work. Today I want you to take stock of how far you've come, to consider where you were when you began and where you are today.

Do you remember that slip of paper that you put in an envelope before Day 14, just over two weeks ago? I had asked you to write down a single goal for the kind of shift you hoped to create in your life as a result of doing this vibrational work. Perhaps this shift was subtle. Perhaps it was dramatic. It may have involved your finances, or your family life, or simply the way you navigate your emotional landscape.

I'd like for you to go find that envelope now. I hope you kept it handy. Now is the moment to take stock of how far you've come. This is a moment of quiet reflection that will give you an opportunity to see a before-and-after picture of where you were then—and where you are now.

Go ahead. Dig that envelope out of its hiding place. I'll wait right here.

Got it?

Good.

What does this before-and-after picture tell you? You may have a greater level of self-love. Or self-confidence. Perhaps you have more abundance and opportunity. Here you have the opportunity to see the distance you've traveled. And through doing this, you can give yourself a pat on the back.

We need to take the time to acknowledge where we've come from. I remember, when I was first working out, trying to do things that I couldn't even begin to do. I felt like a ninety-eight-pound weakling. It was embarrassing! But after a steady period of working out, I was able to do all of the exercises and then some. I could run the distances. Lift the weights. It wasn't easy—but that hard work and dedication led me places I couldn't have imagined.

As you move through your day, receive this news of how far you've come. We don't tend to take the time to do this. We don't celebrate our own accomplishments. Maybe you're not as angry. Or judgmental. Or lazy. Or anxious. *The lens through which you view yourself has been altered.* Being able to see this will give you a sense of pride and accomplishment. Really take it in: *Wow, I did that! That's amazing! I did that!*

Carry this feeling with you into your day. This understanding of your own growth allows you to further accelerate your ability. You've proven to yourself that you've accomplished something that felt beyond the realm of possibility.

So now you know.

And you can expand.

You can do even more.

More space will continue to open inside you and around you as you keep doing this vibrational work.

Go ahead and tuck that slip of paper back into its envelope. Put it back in the drawer where you found it. It's a wonderful touchstone—a reminder that you can continue to grow and evolve. It is a measure of the steps you've climbed on the spiral staircase.

NIGHT

There is nothing else you need to do. Nowhere to be. No one to call. No plans to make. Everything you need has taken root in you. Now it is time to be still and quiet. To listen to your breath. To listen to the child within. To allow everything that you have remembered about your own true and essential nature to grow and flower within you.

All of the ingredients are present.

Just as roots take hold in the fertile earth, just as they grow and spread slowly in the quiet dark, so does our life's path grow and spread of its own accord, in the fullness of time.

We cannot force change.

We cannot force illumination.

What we can do is prepare ourselves by growing ever more present, ever more connected to the Divine in all things. Ever more intuitive and conscious of our own true nature.

We don't have to work at it.

We have to abide within it.

We don't have to strive.

We have to *be*.

We must trust that in being—in inhabiting ourselves on every possible level—we will be placing ourselves in the path of untold and unimagined opportunity. We are accelerating our ability to fully live our lives.

We think we know what is best for us. We think we know what we want. But whenever we think we know, we are, in fact, selling ourselves short.

Stop trying.

Stop striving.

Stop working.

As you sleep tonight, you are like those roots of a beautiful young tree, spreading in the fragrant earth. Those roots are taking hold. They are being nourished. They will grow and grow until you are the stately and magnificent expression of all that you are meant to be.

Imagine it. All you have to do is sleep. All you have to do in the morning is simply be awake. Aware. Connected.

And greet the day with love.

DAY 31 Be the Change

MORNING

So many of us believe that we have to *do something:* We have to take action in order to make a difference in the world. We must have a higher purpose, a mission, a profound calling. And while action certainly has its place, it's really *how we are* in the world that makes the difference. Consider this: If you are at peace with yourself, you are already making a difference. We can donate money, or send aid, or volunteer at a shelter, but the first thing we must do is to take responsibility and stock of our own path of consciousness.

If you come into harmony with yourself and vibrate from that out into the world, you are de facto change. It's not about magnitude. It's not about the grand nature of the contribution externally. *If you gather up all the parts of yourself and love them, that love becomes contagious.* The ripple effect of this kind of energy is tremendous—in some ways more profound than all the external contributions that have ever been made. Because the more we are at peace with ourselves, the more our collective energy will shift, and anything that stands in the way of that peace and tranquility will have no choice but to end or dissolve.

Feel everything inside you. Come to a place of peace. You are becoming a part of the ever-expanding minority. We want as many hubs of peace on this earth as possible. When the consciousness changes, we undergo a paradigm shift. And every single person reading this book is playing a part in that paradigm shift—out of fear and into love.

Completion. Peace. These are the seeds you will be sowing. Don't rush to *do* something. Just sit still. Allow yourself to be the change. There's no effort involved. Eventually there will be time for action. This path isn't about complacency, after all. You can get on a plane later—once you know yourself better. But for now your willingness to walk this journey is, in and of itself, enough.

NOON

Maybe this morning you woke up on the wrong side of bed. You can just feel it internally when this happens. And it can happen even after thirty days of self-awareness. Nothing's right. You're grumpy. You had a bad dream. Your husband snored. Your back aches. Whatever the reason: Now you have the awareness as well as the tools to *turn this around*. You have an entire vibrational universe at your disposal—and you can shift in an instant out of fear and into love.

Be the change.

Be the solution.

Every single moment you feel challenged today, embrace the opportunity to be the change.

Each interaction.

Each person.

Each situation.

When you feel stuck.

When something feels off.

Approach it all, ready to be your clearest, least-encumbered self.

Look within. Feel the ripples of dissonance inside you. What are you feeling beyond the vague sense of something not being right? When that gray storm cloud is hovering over your head, what's really happening? Is it fear? Anger? *You won't have to look very far.* You won't have to go hunting for it. You'd better believe it's right there.

If you commit powerfully to serenity, you will be willing to quickly see the density that's stopping you, and that density will begin to crumble. You will be the mountain still standing after the avalanche: majestic, tall, in one piece. Let it all fall away. If you're committed to *being the change*, this means that you are committed to serenity. You won't sacrifice that serenity for anything or anybody.

As you navigate your day, as you move through challenges, stories, and the dramas around you, you can do so by identifying and feeling everything inside you and flowing through it, back to the bedrock of peace.

That peace will emanate out from you, surrounding and touching everything in your path. In this way, you will be effecting change wherever you go. Whatever you do. Whomever you encounter.

Remember that it starts with you.

NIGHT

The world will wait for you. Problems will still exist tomorrow. The injustice, prejudice, war, famine, child labor, homelessness, racism, homophobia—it isn't going anywhere. Not yet. Not today.

You feel all the sorrows of the world in your heart.

You want to reach out. To lend a hand. To help in any way you can.

And you will. When you're ready. When you understand what role you need to play. When you are so completely clear of any personal motivations that your path is simply laid out for you. In order for this to happen, first you must address your own conflicts. Your own disputes. Your own intimate wars.

You're nearly there. You're practically at the mountaintop. From here, you are so close to being the change the world needs from you. The beauty of this path is that once you are clear of the vibrational density that has held you in place, you cannot help but become part of the solution.

That's all there is left to do.

Once you've embraced all that you are, once you've come into a place of peace, all that is left to do is share yourself.

Give yourself away.

Give yourself to as many people as possible.

You will not be seeking to become complete by rescuing others. You already are complete.

Love is the only thing left.

Tonight, as you turn out the lights, know that a day will come when you will be called into contribution. You will know it when it happens. You will recognize it—in the same way that you have learned to recognize your messengers. You won't wonder if you should or shouldn't. You won't question your motives.

You will simply—with grace and dignity, and fullness of heart—do what needs to be done.

But not tonight. Tonight, it's time to go to sleep.

Day 32 **Being an Instrument**

MORNING

Art flows through all great artists. Composers, painters, sculptors, poets—when they are producing their greatest work, they are acting as channels for the Divine. They forgo their own egoic needs in order to harness the power of the soul. We cannot understand or undergo this experience by using our minds. It simply cannot be understood that way. All great things are born of the heart. As this Density Detox nears the end, you have begun to come into harmony with yourself—and, in so doing, you are poised to access the immeasurable power that every single person who has made a difference on this planet has accessed since the beginning of time.

Before this starts to make you nervous—you know, *Who, me? Immeasurable power?*—please let me assure you that the universe has a safety mechanism in all this, a foolproof way to ensure that this power can be used only for the greater good. You must come into harmony with yourself before you can access this immeasurable power. It doesn't work otherwise.

Through coming into harmony with yourself, it's no longer about you! You are the instrument. We are all instruments—and the maestro is the Divine. This greatest of all conductors wants to orchestrate this wonderful melody through us—but in order for that melody to be seen and heard, we must come into harmony with ourselves.

Every human being possesses the ability to have this happen. And not just for moments but as the moment-to-moment experience of our life.

By virtue of the fact that you've had the courage to walk this walk with me, you've begun to unlock the infinite power and expression of who you really are. You have realized throughout these different detoxifying steps that the universe is on your side. You're not living in an adversarial reality. You're living in a reality in which *everything wants you to win. To have greater abundance. To navigate your life with grace and ease.* Trust this. And when you falter, remember the universal wise words of St. Francis and ask the Divine to make you an instrument of peace. There is tremendous freedom in this. You've done all the exercises. You've embarked on the journey. At this point, you have a real-life understanding of what this has been about. You have navigated all the way to the very depths of yourself.

NOON

You are ready. As we near the end of the active part of this vibrational work, you have come to a place where you can consciously, methodically feel the energy flowing through you.

At this moment, I'm going to ask you to take a few minutes to really feel this happening. Put down your mug of coffee or tea. Settle yourself in your chair. You are open. More open than you've ever allowed yourself to be. This openness is what will allow you to recognize and experience the flow of energy that is *always moving through you.* Just as music flows through a musician, just as words flow through a writer, just as a painter's brush moves almost of its own volition on the canvas, life wants to move through you.

You, too, are an instrument. You've honed this instrument. You've polished it. You've brought out its patina. You've lovingly taken care of it. *Now it's time to use it.* You could be a street sweeper, a bank manager, a housewife, a college student. It doesn't matter what you do. Allow yourself to open. Feel what's happening in your body. What is arising within you? You may feel chills. You may feel something akin to a wave. Pinpricks. Breathe. Relax.

Allow. Invite this connection. You may feel heat. Or a swelling within you. Keep breathing.

Say: *I am open to receive.*

I am ready to be this instrument.

The very moment you invite this connection, it's as if a switch has been turned on. Grace comes flooding in. Inspiration comes flooding in. Higher wisdom comes flooding in.

Love.

Peace.

All of this lives inside you.

Make this conscious connection. You can do this every day, moving forward. *Tune in.* Throughout your day, come back to this place. Over and over again, return to this feeling. Connect. *Don't push against life.* When you push against life, life refuses to unfold. *Allow grace to lead the way.*

Come home.

Come to this place of asking, allowing, receiving.

Everything within you shifts when you become willing to be open.

Let go.

Be an instrument.

NIGHT

We are all instruments in the great and all-encompassing orchestra of the Divine. Each of us has a different melody, a different register, different notes to play. Imagine that you are a flute. Not just any ordinary flute but a gorgeous, ancient, engraved work of art. It gleams with a patina all its own. This is a flute that has been here since the beginning of time.

You are that flute.

You inhabit it. Embody it.

Every breath you take is another note that the Divine is playing. Every breath is part of the vast orchestra—mingling with other instruments. Becoming one with all of the other breaths in the world.

Be the flute.

Be that breath.

Feel the ease with which each inhalation and exhalation moves through your body. Feel the breath in your belly. In your chest. In your throat. In your nostrils.

Allow the music to form through you. It has the quality of a love song: plaintive, haunting. Allow the notes to ring out. Attune yourself to the sound of these notes. The sound of this breath. There is nothing more unique or beautiful.

Only you can play this melody. Only you are this particular instrument. Your stories—the whole of your life as you have experienced it—create the precise tonal quality. It is unlike any other.

Be that breath.

Make the music only you can play.

Give yourself over to it. All of it.

By now you trust that the Divine is present to support

you in every imaginable way. With each note—with each unimpeded, open, trusting breath—you are moving into greater levels of transparency.

Your vibrational density falls away like chunks of mortar.

This breath is the music of the Divine.

The Divine has never been more present than at this very moment.

Day 33 Love

Here we are, my friends. We are coming to the end—which is really just a leaping-off point into magnificence. We now reside in a place of authenticity, where we are able to experience and articulate love. When I first encountered the Divine, this was what I discovered, and I am merely today's messenger, here to pass along with absolute clarity that the key to unlocking yourself and the world around you can be summed up in this one simple word:

Love.

When I speak around the world, I end my programs with the phrase: *I love you and thank you for loving me.*

I love you and thank you for loving me.

Because ultimately it all boils down to this one single sentence. What else can possibly be said, when we see the truth of the Divine in everything and everyone? When we have come to realize that everything and everyone we see is a fragment or a particle of the Divine? What else can you possibly say?

You've done it. I've provided you with the platform, but you've done it! Your willingness has brought you to this experience and this point. You have begun to walk, one step at a time, across the mighty bridge from victimhood to empowerment.

You have examined your fear, your sadness, your anger, your guilt, and your shame. You have delved into your patterns and addictions. You have faced the insatiable needs of your ego. You have identified your self-sabotage and the triggers that get in your way. You have found your breath. You have surrendered. You have become more loving, more spacious. You've climbed a step or two up the infinite spiral staircase.

You have made the journey from fear to love!

This is the journey you have walked.

You've gone from something sharp and spiky to a beautiful soft blanket that you can wrap around yourself at any given moment. You have softened into yourself.

This blanket is invisible.

From a distance you might look exactly the same.

But you know it's there—and, trust me, it's there for good.

Internally, everything has shifted. Everything has changed.

You've been born into yourself.

NOON

So often we live our lives for others. We care for our families. We support our husbands and wives. We raise our children. We're there for our friends. We bring food when our neighbors are sick. We volunteer at our local homeless shelter. We donate to the Red Cross.

But where are we in all of this? Where is all of that bountiful, magnificent love when it comes to our own private selves?

This thing called love reveals itself in so many different ways. We are good at loving parts of ourselves—but not so good at loving *all that we are.* We embrace our best qualities and close our eyes to what we consider to be the worst. Our shame. Our anger. Our pain. Our sorrow. And so we stint. We are stingy with ourselves in a way we would never be with our closest loved ones. Imagine the way a mother cares for her newborn child. Can you imagine treating yourself with such focus and generosity and reverence? Such compassion and kindness?

Here are some crucial questions: Are we feeding ourselves? With whom are we surrounding ourselves? How are we choosing to show up in each moment? What is the tone of our inner voice? Is it an angry teacher? Or a beneficent presence?

Just for today, focus on the way you love yourself. This is not a selfish thing to do. On the contrary: It is the greatest gift you can offer to everyone in your life. The more you are filled with love, the more you can be available to everyone around you in a spacious, gracious way.

Just for today, know that you deserve your own love.

Fill yourself as if you're the most beautiful china bowl.

Fill and refill yourself with this love. There is no end to it.

NIGHT

Where does love begin? Is there a starting place? A seed that is planted somewhere, then grows into something we can feel and see? Does love have a house? Does love have a face? A body? A voice? A form?

Love exists.

Love has always existed.

Love existed before there was an earth. Before there were galaxies. Before anything we know as life came into being. Love is the ocean in which we swim. It is the air we breathe. It permeates every particle, every molecule, every single aspect of our experience.

If we cannot trace love back to its beginnings, then surely we know that *love never ends.*

This is the one constant, never-changing truth of life itself: Love dwells within you. Around you. For you. Through you. Ever-present, available, accessible. It is your guiding principle.

The hand of love has touched your life from its inception. That hand has never wavered. It gently ushers you on. It offers you support and guidance. It comforts you. It points you in directions you never would have dreamed of.

You are holding the very last pages of this book.

This book itself is love.

The hand that turns the page is not separate from the page. The reader and the words are one and the same.

As you sleep tonight—the sound sleep of one who is filled with peace and contentment—know that love is all around you. And should you for a moment forget that this is the case, you need look no further than within.

The end is really just the beginning.

I love you and thank you for loving me.

Acknowledgments

To the indispensable JC Carpenter and everyone at Panache Desai, LLC for their tireless dedication and support.

To my wonderful agent, Jennifer Rudolph Walsh, and the entire team at William Morris Endeavor.

To the outrageously talented Julie Grau and the entire Penguin Random House family for their dedication, support, and commitment.

To the sweet soul and my dear friend Dani Shapiro.

To the personification of Soul Signature that is Oprah Winfrey for her inspiration, generosity, and graciousness.

And finally, to you, the reader. Thank you for allowing me the honor of a lifetime, of guiding you back to your true self. May the end of this book mark the beginning of a life greater than you have ever known.

ABOUT THE AUTHOR

PANACHE DESAI is a contemporary thought leader whose message of love and self-acceptance has drawn thousands of people from around the world to his seminars and workshops. He is on the faculty of the Omega Institute and the Kripalu Center for Yoga & Health. This is his first book.

ABOUT THE TYPE

The text of this book was set in Janson, a typeface designed about 1690 by Nicholas Kis (1650–1702), a Hungarian living in Amsterdam, and for many years mistakenly attributed to the Dutch printer Anton Janson. In 1919, the matrices became the property of the Stempel Foundry in Frankfurt. It is an oldstyle book face of excellent clarity and sharpness. Janson serifs are concave and splayed; the contrast between thick and thin strokes is marked.